HISTORIC CANADA

HISTORIC CANADA

Kildare Dobbs
and Marjorie Harris

METHUEN
Toronto   New York   London   Sydney   Auckland

Copyright © 1984 Discovery Books

Discovery Books, 70 The Esplanade, Toronto, Ontario, Canada M5E 1R2

ISBN 0-458-98530-9

Produced by Discovery Books, Toronto for:
Methuen Publications,
2330 Midland Avenue,
Agincourt, Ontario M1S 1P7

Maps: Emma Hess
Research: John Wellwood
Design: Joanna Gertler

Printed and bound in Italy by Sagdos S.p.A.

➜ PHOTOGRAPHIC CREDITS ⬳

Jim Challoner 82 upper left

John de Visser 15, 19, 22-3, 26-7, 30-1, 32, 34, 35, 42 upper, 54, 59, 67, 70-1, 82 left and upper right, 91 upper left, 94 upper right, 95, 106 upper and lower left, 107, 110 left, 111, 114-5, 124-5, 140-1, 146 upper right, 147, 152 upper left and right, 161, 172 upper left and lower right, 177, 184 upper and lower right

Kildare Dobbs 66

Department of Regional Industrial Expansion 146 upper left, 148-9, 172 upper left, 196, 197

Horst Ehricht 46, 78-9, 83, 94 lower right, 121, 154-5, 146 left, 168-9, 173

Menno Fieguth 180, 197

Owen Fitzgerald 47

L.A. Morse 55

Birgitte Nielsen 43, 110 upper and lower right, 118-9, 128, 136, 176

Parks Canada 42 left

Paul von Baich 74-5, 91 lower left, 94 upper and lower left, 98-9, 137, 160, 164-5, 172 upper left, 184 upper and lower left, 185, 188-9, 192-3, 200

Richard Vroom 38-9, 50, 51, 62-3, 86-7, 90, 102-3, 106 right, 129 upper and lower, 148-9, 153

Ted Yarwood 132-3

Glenbow Archives 154 lower, 171 upper

Metropolitan Toronto Library 32, 36, 37, 49 lower, 72 lower, 76, 85, 93, 96 upper and lower, 108, 109, 112, 116, 120 lower, 126 upper and lower, 130, 131, 135, 139, 143, 147, 150 lower, 154 upper, 171 lower

Public Archives of Canada 13, 24 lower, 28, 29, 33, 40, 44, 45, 48, 49 upper, 52, 53, 57, 60, 61, 64, 77, 81 lower, 84, 88 upper and lower, 89, 100, 104, 105, 113 upper and lower, 120 upper, 122, 134, 146 upper and lower, 151, 155, 158 lower, 159 upper and lower, 167, 170, 174, 175, 187 upper and lower, 190, 191 upper, 194 upper and lower, 195

Royal Ontario Museum 8, 17, 24 upper, 72 upper, 80, 81 upper, 92, 97, 117, 123, 127, 142, 150 upper, 154 lower, 158 upper, 162, 166, 178, 182, 186, 191 lower

Frontispiece
Bonsecours Market, Montreal
(Horst Ehricht)
Title page
Old Murray Premises, St. John's
(John de Visser)
Dance Hall Girls, Barkerville
(Menno Fieguth)

Overleaf
The *Bluenose*, off Halifax
(John de Visser)

St. Paul's Church, Halifax, Nova Scotia

HISTORIC CANADA

THE MOVEMENT OF ASIATIC PEOPLES into what is now Canada was from west to east in prehistoric times. They began coming some 40,000 years ago across the Aleutian land bridge. And they kept coming, though the number of those who stayed was probably never more than 300,000 or 400,000. Most of them passed through on their way south to evolve the high civilizations of Central and South America, the precarious cultures of the Amazonian rain forests and the techniques of bare survival in Tierra del Fuego.

In Canada the material culture of most of these peoples was perishable; they left few traces of their passing. But here and there across the enormous land are found mysterious evidences of their religion and art: petroglyphs, rock paintings, serpent mounds and cairns.

By the time they entered recorded history, they had developed Neolithic cultures, spoke at least nine distinct languages and, on the Pacific coast where the climate was mild, had created a sophisticated culture whose art has been favourably compared with that of ancient Greece. Hardly less impressive was the political organization of the eastern tribes; the Iroquois Confederation was a model of statesmanship and military acumen.

The historical record begins with the coming of literate Europeans from the east, and with them moves slowly westward. Because of this gradual westward penetration of the continent, following the river beds, different regions of modern Canada have different time scales. In Calgary or Edmonton 100 years ago seems antiquity; in Quebec it is the day before yesterday.

About A.D. 1000 the Viking Leif Ericsson discovered certain barren countries to the west of Greenland which he called Helluland and Markland. Then he established a colony on a more fertile shore, naming it Vinland. Scholarly conjecture identifies the first two places as Baffin Island and Labrador, while the discovery of the remains of a Viking settlement at L'Anse aux Meadows, Newfoundland, suggests the probable site of Vinland. The colony was short lived.

Over the next five centuries fishermen from western Europe must have begun visiting the Grand Banks off Newfoundland to exploit the prodigal abundance of cod. Some of them probably landed to dry-cure the catches, which, in the form of *bacalao*, or stockfish, became an important food staple in Europe. If so, they kept quiet about it. Not until the 15th century, when rival European powers were seeking new routes to the rich Oriental trade, did professional navigators trumpet their discoveries. Sailing westward on a strange new theory that the earth was a globe, Columbus came on the islands of the Caribbean and claimed an empire for Spain.

France and Britain, now rivals in the discovery race, began to contend for empire in North America. In 1497 John Cabot sighted Newfoundland and claimed it for England. In 1534 Jacques Cartier, a Breton from Saint-Malo, came to the Gaspé, setting up cross and *fleur-de-lys* to signify that the country belonged to the king of France.

For the next 250 years Britain and France would fight for control of Canada. A series of forts from Cape Breton to Thunder Bay bears witness to that long struggle. Some of these forts — for example France's strategic Louisbourg on Cape Breton, commanding the entrance to the St. Lawrence, and Britain's Fort Prince of Wales at Churchill, both mighty strongholds in their day — fell to attackers without resistance and were razed to the ground. Later, stone by stone, they were piously rebuilt as Canadian monuments.

The French were the first to succeed in colonizing the new country, beginning with the settlement at Port Royal on the Bay of Fundy. It was well situated for fishing and farming but vulnerable to attack by hostile Indians and, in time, by the aggressive British colonists from New England who captured and renamed it Annapolis. But it was the colony around Quebec, founded in 1608, that proved to be the enduring centre of French power in Canada.

Europeans had come to these shores for the cod fisheries. They stayed to trade for furs. Tribesmen, who had hitherto heated water in wooden vessels by dropping hot stones into it, were insatiable in their demand for copper kettles. They also craved steel knives, awls, hatchets and other tools and weapons to replace their flint and stone; blankets and cloth, needles, thread, beads, buttons; and above all firearms, powder and ball. Nor did it take them long to develop a discriminating taste for French brandy. In return for these precious goods, the natives gave their greasy old beaver coats and all the other pelts they could collect.

For Europeans, these furs, especially beaver, were excellent objects of trade. Like the spices of the Indies, they were easy to carry and ship and in high demand in Europe. Beaver was ideal for making felt hats, which stayed in fashion until the invention of the silk shag hat in 1798. And furs had been in short supply in the capitals of Europe since the Turks had blocked the trade routes from Muskovy.

The French colony founded by Samuel de Champlain at Quebec controlled the St. Lawrence trade, making allies of the Hurons, who became the middlemen in the traffic upcountry. Their competitors were first the Dutch, then the English on the Hudson River system, which was controlled by their allies, the Iroquois. Iroquois raids compelled the French to build a post at Montreal in 1642, and a fort at the mouth of the Richelieu, where the river route from New York cut into the St. Lawrence. Nevertheless, in the summer of 1648, Iroquois raiders penetrated to the Huron villages near Georgian Bay and destroyed them, killing a Jesuit missionary and returning the following summer to murder four more and massacre the Hurons. The blood of the martyrs was the seed of the church; French Canadians never forgot Brébeuf and his brethren, faithful unto death by torture.

The more immediate catastrophe was the destruction of the Huron nation, and the threat to the infant colony at Quebec. The Acadian colony changed hands more than once but was restored to France in 1670. Meanwhile, in 1663, New France was brought under royal authority.

It was to be a regular French province, with French institutions transplanted to the new world: a governor from the nobility; an intendant from the bourgeois bureaucracy; a bishop answerable to the French hierarchy. The image of prerevolutionary France was completed by a feudal land system, with *habitants* obedient to their pastors and seigneurial masters. A crack regiment of France now stormed into the bush, vainly striving to bring the elusive Iroquois to action. The soldiers did succeed, though, in devastating crops, settlements and granaries, frightening the Indians so badly that they sued for peace.

Except for the show of force, none of this was much use to the fur trade, which, as an enterprise of hunters and nomads, was always at odds with the life of peasants tied to the land by chores and feudalism. The peasants settled in to breed.

More restless spirits succumbed to the lure of the wild river, with its promise of adventure, riches and free love. These *coureurs de bois* came to know and admire the natives, adopting the canoe, the showshoe, the sled, along with a stoical tolerance of cruelty, pain and hardship. The colonial authorities, especially the bishop, frowned on these lewd, flashy fellows, "prodigal not only in their Cloaths, but upon Women."

Two outstandingly tough specimens of the breed were so enraged by their treatment in Quebec that they deserted the colony. Radisson and Groseilliers defected to England with a scheme to bypass the French colonies and trade directly with the Indians of the interior. Their plan was to send ships into Hudson Bay and set up posts, or "factories," far to the north of the French. Fired by this proposal, which intrigued Charles II and his more scientific courtiers, the world's most enduring trading corporation was launched in 1670 with a royal charter, Prince Rupert as governor, and the heroic title, "The Governor and Company of Adventurers of England trading into Hudson's Bay."

The Hudson's Bay Company began with the hope of profit. Vigorous promotion by Pierre Radisson and his comrade, whom the English called Mister Gooseberry, promised no less.

But the French, already beset by New England colonists, reacted fiercely to this new threat from the north. The great names of Count Frontenac, La Salle and D'Iberville testify to the powerful westward drive of French enterprise and exploration, and their savage onslaughts on English factories. For 28 years, from 1690 until 1718, the English company paid no dividends. Even then, it was diplomacy rather than military virtue that enabled them to resume profitable trade. The Treaty of Utrecht gave them back their factories.

Their royal charter had enjoined them to seek a Northwest Passage to China, and in this they were more active than their critics at home gave them credit for. While the French explorer La Vérendrye reached Rainy Lake only in 1732, where he built Fort St. Charles, young Henry Kelsey of the Hudson's Bay Company had arrived on the prairies as early as 1690, reporting his adventures with the Plains Indians in doggerel verse.

The boy Kelsey was English, but in time the Hudson's Bay Company came to prefer Orkneymen because they were "strictly faithful to their employers" and, better still, "sordidly avaricious." It is hard to see what could have reconciled any man, avaricious or not, to the harsh conditions of the Canadian north, with its brief summers tormented by blackflies and mosquitoes, and its long, dark, bone-chilling winters. Historians are tight-lipped on the subject, but the attraction does seem to have been the easy-going sexual mores of the Indians. "This was certainly that freedom . . . the antient poets dreamed of," a company sea-captain reported. Stories of the happy freedom of the "savages" inspired Jean Jacques Rousseau to base his political philosophy on the notion of the Noble Savage. Such ideas sowed the seeds of revolution

Battle of Chateauguay, 1813

in France and America and of rebellion in Ireland. Meanwhile, commercial rivalry in the westward thrust of the fur trade intensified with the long struggle between France and Britain.

In the end it was British sea power that decided the issue. The Battle of the Plains of Abraham, 1759, in which the redcoats of General Wolfe routed the French columns of General Montcalm is commonly thought of as the hour of conquest. A brief, bloody encounter in which both commanders fell, it left the British in possession of Quebec. But it was the arrival of the Royal Navy in the St. Lawrence the following year that sealed the victory.

Louisbourg had fallen in 1758, leaving the great river open to invaders. Acadia had changed hands again, ceded to Britain by the Treaty of Utrecht on condition that the Roman religion be tolerated (an extraordinary concession for those bigoted times). But the steady refusal of the Acadians to swear allegiance to the Crown had so alarmed the British that they expelled the unlucky *habitants*, dispersing them among other colonies. Many of them later found their way back.

France now abandoned her Canadians to the conqueror, who dealt with the new subjects by a policy of masterly inaction, permitting them to retain their religion and civil law. No one objected to the introduction of English criminal law, with its presumption of innocence. Toleration of the Catholics put the bishop on the side of British authority. In North America, His Britannic Majesty would have few more docile subjects than the French Canadians.

A handful of hungry Scots, along with Yankees and Englishmen, had arrived in Montreal as war contractors. They soon took over the French posts and routes in the fur trade, continuing the time-honoured rivalry between the St. Lawrence and Hudson routes, and challenging the monopoly of the Hudson's Bay Company. The entire fur trade was now in British hands. And yet — same difference! — competition in the westward drive had never been fiercer.

Even though the northern colonies shared many of the grievances that provoked rebellion in the Thirteen Colonies, they remained aloof. Not that they were extravagantly loyal to the Crown. Rather, they were continuing the age-old rivalries going back to the wars between the Iroquois and the Laurentian tribes. And when ragged Yankee armies arrived to liberate Montreal and Quebec they inspired little but dislike.

Montreal grew and prospered on the fur trade. The Hyperborean Nabobs of the St. Lawrence, hard-bitten Scots, rode westward over the rivers and lakes in their *canots de maître*, paddled by cheerful *voyageurs*, the French-Canadian workhorses of the trade. Along the route the men took women and wives "after the custom of the country," begetting dusky broods of half-breeds, or Métis. In time the traders formed a syndicate called the North West Company, bringing together the talents of such organizers as Simon McTavish and Joseph Frobisher and explorers such as Peter Pond, Alexander Mackenzie, who crossed the continent in 1793, and Simon Fraser, who first descended the tumultuous river bearing his name. The Hudson's Bay Company had bred a number of heroes of its own: James Knight, Samuel Hearne and David Thompson. But the magnificent Nor'Westers had given them such a run for their money by 1821, when the London company took them over, that they had made themselves, in Washington Irving's phrase, "lords of the lakes and forests."

An essential feature of the fur trade was that it interfered as little as possible with Indian life and was jealously opposed to homesteading and settlement. And indeed the limitless Pre-Cambrian Shield country that covers most of Canada is utterly intractable to cultivation. In the heroic age of exploration there were no Indian killers, no land stealers. From the beginning, the Hudson's Bay Company had instructed its servants, "You are to use the natives with kindness and civility." Indians and traders were partners.

Violence did sometimes break out between rival traders. A Scottish factor at Cumberland House was obliged to warn an Irish Nor'Wester that "Scots could kill as well as Irishmen." And the practice of treaty trade, by which prices in beaver pelts for trade goods were fixed by agreement between tribal chiefs and trader, sometimes bound the latter to take sides in Indian wars. But warfare was not in the interest of traders. In the literature of exploration there can be few more

British Commissioner's House, St. John's

Quidi Vidi Fort, St. John's

anguished pages than Hearne's account of his helplessness to restrain his Indian comrades from the massacre of defenceless Inuit at the place he called Bloody Falls.

Contact with white men and their technology did, however, have its hazards for Stone Age peoples. They died of new diseases. In their quarrels they could kill more easily with steel weapons and guns than with stone axes. Liquor was a novelty to them, delightful at first, but in the end, as their self-esteem collapsed in the face of massive settlement, a false refuge.

The victory of the American rebels brought a flood of Loyalist refugees to the northern colonies. These early boat people, some 40,000 of them, carried a new strain of conservatism to British America, already a region wary of change. Most Canadians were now people who had been on the wrong side of two revolutions, the French and the American. Like Andrew Marvell, the English poet who had taken the Puritan side in the Civil War, they tended to feel that "the cause was too good to have been fought for. . . . Men ought to have trusted the King with the whole matter."

The Hudson's Bay Company now traded alone in its immense territory, which included most of what is now Canada from Labrador to the Pacific, as well as the Oregon Territory. Sir George Simpson ruled supreme. Travelling by express canoe with picked *voyageurs,* or gliding over the snows in his magnificent cabriole, the Little Emperor visited and harried the factories from Montreal to Nootka Sound, always accompanied by his piper.

Yet the fur trade was shrinking before the relentless advance of settlements, with its attendant destruction of Indians and wildlife.

Now it was the lumber trade that had become the high road to adventure, romance and quick riches. In the last age of wooden ships, the forests of Nova Scotia and New Brunswick supplied the munitions and sinews of sea power; not only spars, masts, tar and turpentine for the warships based in Halifax, but up to one-third of the vessels in the British merchant marine, then the largest in the world. And in the wooden walls sailed the hearts of oak, the seafaring men of the Atlantic.

On the west coast, Captain James Cook had sailed into Nootka Sound in 1778; and in 1792 Captain George Vancouver had arrived to confirm Britain's claim to the region over that of Spain.

Relations with the neighbour republic were uneasy after Independence. They broke out in violence in the War of 1812. The victories of General Isaac Brock at Detroit and Queenston Heights, where he was killed leading a charge, raised Canadian self-esteem. Local militia fought alongside British regulars (mostly Irish) and Indian allies and provided a much needed hero in the person of James FitzGibbon, who received the surrender of a large body of Americans at Niagara.

Neither side won the war. If the Yankees succeeded in burning Fort York (now Toronto), the British and Canadians put the torch to Washington, gutting the White House. Canadians now knew they could give as good as they got.

Imperial London had learned nothing from its American experience, or next to nothing. The Empire, an Irish wit was to observe, was an

The Lower Market, Quebec City

enormous system of outdoor relief for the upper classes. From resistance to foppish officials and placemen grew the novel idea of Responsible Government, most eloquently expounded by the Nova Scotia journalist Joseph Howe. First Halifax, then other capitals insisted on legislatures based on this principle.

Explosions of frustration in Upper and Lower Canada (Ontario and Quebec) in the 1830s merely confirmed the Canadian feeling that political violence was disreputable. The population was growing and changing with successive waves of immigration. The famine Irish of the 1840s, Orange as well as Green, were adding their fractious voices to those of the so-called founding races, yet there was tacit agreement that constitutional means were the way to Responsible Government, Reform and Independence.

Britain, however, was nervous about Canada. The Civil War showed American readiness for war. The Fenian raids in the 1860s proved that in a nation born of blood any gang of fanatics could justify violence. The Fenians, Irish nationalists who longed to strike a blow at the British oppressor by attacking Canada, confirmed Canadian disgust with rebels. To Westminster, though, it looked as if American annexationism were still a threat. Heavy fortifications had been built in the first half of the century at Halifax, Quebec and Kingston, as well as a number of strategic canals. The cost of imperial security was frightening. A movement toward national sentiment would be welcome.

It came in the form of Confederation in 1867. The Fathers of Confederation who met in Charlottetown, Prince Edward Island, in 1864, were colonial delegates at whose request Westminster enacted the new constitution. By the British North America Act of 1867 four of the scattered colonies of British America became provinces of the new, self-governing Dominion of Canada. Like the mother country, Canada was now a constitutional monarchy in which the (absentee) Crown, represented by the governor general, was the symbol of authority. But the Parliament that exercised the real power in the new federal capital at Ottawa would share its responsibilities with provincial legislatures.

Canada's immense territories could never have become one nation without modern communications. Building the Canadian Pacific Railway to link British Columbia with the eastern provinces was the new country's first great enterprise. It was built by a collaboration between public and private enterprise, spiced with a little scandal and corruption, that was to become the Canadian way in many national endeavours.

The Hudson's Bay Company surrendered its territories in 1869. Homesteaders began to arrive on the prairie. The Métis, seeing their free nomadic life threatened, rose in revolt. Troops and hangmen arrived by train to restore order, followed by redcoats of the North West Mounted Police. Around the turn of the new century wave after wave of immigrants overran the plains, about one-fifth of them from eastern Europe. Cities and towns sprang up as the region became one of the great wheat-producing areas of the world.

Of necessity, the far-flung country became a pioneer in communications. Railways and telegraphs followed the old trade routes. Alexander Graham Bell invented the telephone in Nova Scotia. Marconi made his first transmissions in Newfoundland.

In the early 20th century the Empire was still a focus of identity for many English-speakers. "I am an imperialist," wrote Stephen Leacock, "because I will not be a colonial." In Quebec language and religion were cherished as symbols of nationhood. The province took pride in being more Catholic than the pope. These attachments to external yet universal institutions, Church and Empire, may have reflected a certain lack of confidence in Canada. As Canadian imperialists marched eagerly to war in South Africa, French Canadians — always excepting the Nile Voyageurs — enlisted in the Papal Zouaves to resist Garibaldi.

It was the extraordinary performance of Canadian soldiers and airmen in the two world wars that first gave this normally unmilitary people pride in their national heritage. True, in peace time, especially after World War II, the pride tended to become a secret, hard to share with the flood of new immigrants, many of them former enemies. A secure sense of national community would have to grow out of shared cultural achievement. It was precisely this distinctive culture that was threatened by the blaring of foreign obsessions over the air waves.

In 1982, Westminster, once more at Ottawa's request, enacted a Canadian constitution, endorsed by all the provinces except Quebec. This time the statute could be amended or repealed only in Canada. The Canadian passion for legitimacy was satisfied, but the quest for national integrity was not ended. It would continue into the new age of technology. There would be a second chance for Canada.

St. Paul's Anglican Church, Harbour Grace

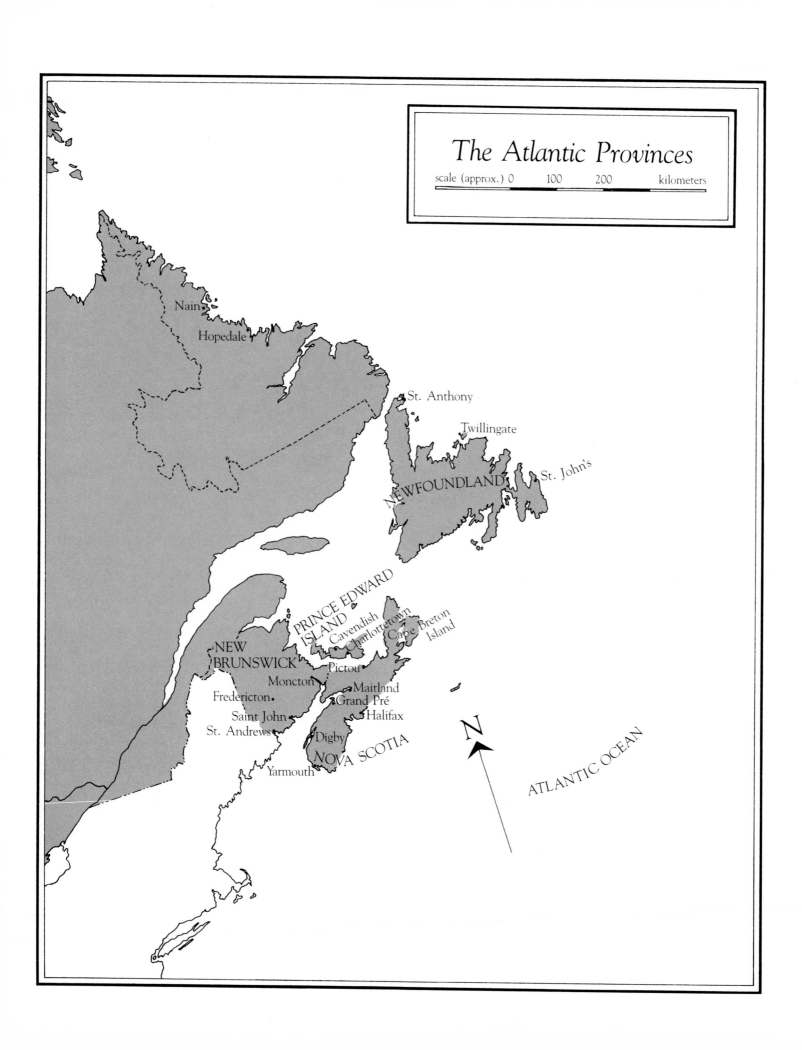

The Atlantic Provinces

scale (approx.) 0   100   200   kilometers

Nain

Hopedale

St. Anthony

Twillingate

St. John's

NEWFOUNDLAND

PRINCE EDWARD
ISLAND

Cavendish
Charlottetown
Cape Breton
Island

NEW
BRUNSWICK

Pictou

Moncton

Maitland

Fredericton

Grand Pré

Saint John

Halifax

St. Andrews

Digby

Yarmouth

NOVA SCOTIA

N

ATLANTIC OCEAN

NEWFOUNDLAND

Newfoundland (pronounced Newf'nd*land*) was proud of being the oldest British colony until 1949, when it became the last Canadian province to enter Confederation. Some islanders still refer to the mainland as Canada, recalling the old song:
Come near at your peril, Canadian Wolf!

Though claimed for Britain in 1497, this doughty rock in the rough North Atlantic yielded only slowly to permanent settlement by migrants, French in some areas, but mostly from the English West Country and the south of Ireland, whose accents may still be detected in island dialects. Many came because of a law that British ships carry a certain number of "boys," or green seamen, a rule made to ensure a supply of trained sailors for the Royal Navy. "Boys" from Devon and Cornwall and Waterford often stayed on the island after a season of work curing fish, having splurged their passage money.

Traditionally Newfoundlanders have been fishermen and sealers. Since the staple is cod from the nearby Grand Banks, the word "fish" here is used exclusively for cod. Before Confederation the social structure of Newfoundland was simple. Wealth and power were in the hands of a small establishment of old families in St. John's, British by education and outlook. Most islanders lived in more or less isolated outports, scraping a livelihood by fishing and farming.

The fine, sheltered harbour of St. John's has long been a refuge for foreign fishing fleets. In two world wars it was a base for British and Canadian warships escorting convoys from North American ports to beleaguered Britain.

From St. John's, a city of painted timber houses with some grand public buildings in stone and concrete, the Trans-Canada Highway runs to Corner Brook, connected by ferries with the mainland.

The province includes the mainland territory of Labrador, a region of barren rocks and mountains that most Canadians view only from the air, and with a shudder. Though provincial law knows no such person as an Indian, there are tribesmen here and there in Labrador. For many years they saw few white men other than the staff of the Grenfell Mission and the occasional fisherman on the coast. Later there was a powerful American presence at a strategic air command base at Goose Bay. Now there are small populations working at various mining camps and the huge hydroelectric installations at Churchill Falls. Visitors are startled to hear Labradoreans speak of St. John's as though it were some remote imperial capital.

Overleaf
View of St. John's

View of St. John's

St. Thomas Church from Government House, St. John's

HISTORIC SITES

ST. JOHN'S

ST. JOHN'S lies in its sheltered harbour, protected from the ravages of the Atlantic by the rocks of Signal Hill. The province once was Britain's oldest colony and this city has some of North America's oldest streets. Its magnificent natural setting is a backdrop for its stirring history.

The Colonial Building was the home of Newfoundland's legislature from 1850 to 1959. It has been restored and it now contains the provincial archives.

Government House is a Georgian-style mansion of rough red sandstone quarried from Signal Hill. Twenty-eight masons, 25 carpenters and a slater were brought from Scotland to do the job. It is now the home of the lieutenant governor.

Anglican Cathedral of St. John is one of the finest examples of ecclesiastical Gothic architecture in North America, with its 25-metre vaulted ceiling. It was designed by Sir Gilbert Scott in the early 19th century and rebuilt after the fire of 1892.

Basilica of St. John the Baptist was built in 1855 in a Romanesque design. The red granite is faced with cut limestone imported from Galway. The mouldings and window frames are of Dublin granite.

Old Garrison Church, Church of St. Thomas is the oldest church still standing in St. John's. Built in 1836, it contains many artifacts from the days when it served the garrison of nearby Fort William.

Signal Hill National Historic Park guards the entrance to the city and harbour of St. John's. It was a natural lookout as early as 1500. This was the site of the last battle of the Seven Years' War in 1762. The Queen's Battery, constructed in the latter half of the 18th century, overlooks the harbour channel and there are remains of a British barracks. Near the Queen's Battery stands the Cabot Tower, built in 1897-98 to commemorate both the 400th anniversary of the discovery of Newfoundland by John Cabot and Queen Victoria's Diamond Jubilee. It occupies the site of a former blockhouse used in the 19th century to signal the arrival of ships.

Quidi Vidi Battery had guns mounted in 1762 to guard the harbour entrance to Quidi Vidi village, which is now part of St. John's. The fort has been restored to the 1812 period.

ST. JOHN'S AREA

BRIGUS, once a great cod fishing town, is located at the head of Conception Bay. In 1847, 2,000 men in 66 vessels went sealing from the town. It is the birthplace of Bob Bartlett, the renowned Arctic navigator who aided Edwin Peary on a number of his voyages.

Cape Spear National Historic Park is the most easterly point in North America. The original lighthouse was built in 1836, contains 19 rooms and has been restored to the 1838-40 period. The two-storey wooden structure is one of the oldest lighthouses in the country. It was replaced by a new lighthouse, which stands nearby, in 1955.

FERRYLAND was once the location of a colony founded by Sir George Calvert, the first Lord Baltimore, in 1621. The family coat of arms is in an old stone church here. Baltimore built an

elegant yellow brick mansion here, but, discouraged by the harsh weather, moved to Maryland in 1634.

Isle of Bois, at the mouth of Ferryland's harbour, still holds the half-buried cannon that defended the town during its most turbulent period. In 1612, Peter Easton, a pirate admiral, and 1,000 fishermen controlled the western Atlantic. He built the battery at the harbour mouth. He amassed a gigantic fortune raiding the Spanish fleets and left in 1614. The naval guns were installed in 1743, abandoned in 1760 and manned intermittently during the American Revolution and the War of 1812. Evidence remains of an 18th-century fort and magazine built here.

HARBOUR GRACE is one of Newfoundland's oldest towns. It was settled in roughly 1550 and fortified in 1610 by Peter Easton, a notorious English pirate. A plaque marks the site of the first Wesleyan mission in North America, established in 1765. This was also the departure point for early transatlantic flights by such renowned aviators as Wiley Post and Amelia Earhart.

Harbour Grace Courthouse, designed by architect Patrick Kough and constructed in 1830-31, was one of the first courthouses approved by the British government in Newfoundland. Forty merchants of Conception Bay paid for it by voluntary subscription based on the amount of fish caught and shipped from the harbour. It is the oldest such building still in use in Canada.

Harbour Grace Roman Catholic Cathedral was built in 1856. The northern part of the colony was created as a separate diocese with Harbour Grace as its centre. The first bishop, Right Reverend Dr. Dalton, built the cathedral and Bishop Carfagnini completed it c. 1879 with the addition of the cupola and transepts.

OTHER HISTORIC SITES

HEART'S CONTENT was the site of North America's first cable relay station. The first successful transatlantic cable was landed here in 1866, linking Heart's Content with Valentia, Ireland. The station was closed in 1965 and has now been reopened as a museum. The oldest section is furnished as it was when the building was erected in 1873.

Hopedale Mission National Historic Site, Labrador, was established in 1782 when the British government granted permission to the Moravian church to establish this mission. This is the oldest frame building east of Quebec. The buildings on the site include the church, storehouse, a residence and small wooden huts for natives. The Mission at Nain, 160 km to the northwest, was settled in 1771, the year the simple but handsome wooden church was built.

Colonial Building, St. John's

L'Anse aux Meadows National Historic Park is located on a grassy plain at the northernmost tip of the Great Northwest Peninsula. There is evidence of a Viking settlement, c. A.D. 1000, believed to have been founded by Leif Ericsson, where the first European birth in North America likely occurred. Archeological digs have uncovered the remains of six sod houses, a smithy, sauna, cooking pits and household articles. In 1978, the park was declared a UNESCO World Heritage Site to honour its universal appeal.

NEWTOWN: **Barbour House** indicates the style of outport aristocracy in the mid-19th century. The 32-room mansion was built by Benjamin Barbour. His progeny turned out generations of famous sea captains.

PLACENTIA: **Castle Hill National Historic Park** was called Plaisance by the founding French at Fort Royal in 1692. It was used as a base to attack English settlements. The Treaty of Utrecht gave it to England in 1713 and it was renamed Placentia. In the 1720s, the British constructed Fort Frederick and in 1762 the French seized and rebuilt Fort Royal. There are remains of the French and English batteries below the hill, and a wall of stone rubble overlooking the harbour. Fort Royal's interior includes the remains of a guardroom, barracks, powder magazine and a blockhouse.

Overleaf
View of Ferryland

St. James' Cathedral, St. John's

ST. ANTHONY, one of the farthest reaches of the northwest coast, is the headquarters of the Grenfell Mission. Sir Wilfred Grenfell, who began his work with people of the Labrador and Newfoundland coasts in 1893 and died in 1940, is buried here.

Port au Choix National Historic Park, St. Anthony area, is one of Canada's most important prehistoric sites. It's the burial ground of the Maritime Archaic Indians, who inhabited these coasts more than 5,000 years ago. The graves of 100 people were revealed in the late 1960s. These Indians were dubbed the red paint people because their graves were lined with red ochre.

TRINITY has two of Newfoundland's finest wooden churches: an 1833 Roman Catholic chapel and an 1822 Anglican church. The museum, a building of saltbox design built in 1843, contains models and artifacts of the fishing, whaling and sealing industries.

Cape Bonavista was probably where John Cabot first landed in 1497. The lighthouse, built in saltbox style in 1842, contains an 1816 light moved from Harbour Grace. Bonavista is one of the province's oldest and largest fishing communities.

Ireland's Eye, an island in Trinity Bay, is the former site of Traytown, now a ghost town. Several houses in the saltbox style remain and there is a half-ruined white frame church whose cemetery contains the graves of the first settlers.

TWILLINGATE was originally named Toulinguet by the Breton fishermen who frequented the village in the 1700s. One of the oldest buidings here is St. Peter's Anglican Church. The white frame structure was erected between 1842 and 1844. The museum contains Inuit artifacts found at Back Harbour, 2.4 km northwest, thought to be 3,500 years old.

Government House, St. John's

Interior bedroom, British Commissioner's House, St. John's

The Moravian Mission, Nain, Labrador

Old Garrison Church, Church of St. Thomas, St. John's

THE SITE OF THE PRINCE'S LODGE   VIEW AT THE PRINCE'S LODGE.

HALIFAX.—THE PRINCE'S MUSIC HOUSE, BEDFORD BASIN.—FROM SKETCHES BY W. O. CARLISLE.—SEE PAGE 242.

Prince's Music House, Halifax, Nova Scotia

THE MARITIMES

THE MARITIME PROVINCES are Nova Scotia, New Brunswick and Prince Edward Island (formerly Île-Saint-Jean). The region is old-world Canada, a country of seafaring people whose great days were back in the age of sail and wooden ships. Although Charlottetown, capital of Prince Edward Island, is known as the cradle of Confederation, the province did not join Canada until 1873.

Since Confederation was roughly contemporary with the rise of steel ships and the coming of steam (between them the ruination of timber shipbuilding), Maritimers were disgusted to see their wealth vanishing up the new railway line to Quebec and Ontario. Montreal they knew, and Boston they knew, but who were these upstarts in Ottawa and Toronto?

The principal cities of the area are Halifax, N.S., founded as a naval base in 1749, and Saint John, N.B., incorporated as a city in 1785. Despite the explosion of an ammunition ship that devastated the city in 1917, Halifax has many historic buildings, including Province House, the first legislature in Canada, where Joseph Howe expounded the principles of Responsible Government; St. George's Anglican Church, whose building and parish registers date from the 18th

Midday Guns and Citadel Clock Tower, Halifax, Nova Scotia

St. Paul's Church, Halifax, Nova Scotia

century; and the Citadel, a 19th-century fort that today houses a marine museum. The Historic Properties on the harbourfront form a business and recreational centre in an area formerly given over to warehouses and wharves. Saint John, too, is at work on an ambitious restoration programme, renovating what used to be a rundown urban centre. Many fine Victorian buildings have been saved. The smaller capital cities of Fredericton and Charlottetown are also rich in historic buildings and streets.

Almost every village and settlement in the Maritimes is historic. In St. Andrews, N.B., for example, may be seen the house design some of the Loyalist fugitives from Maine brought with them. Elsewhere there are lovingly made reconstructions of past splendours: at Louisbourg, Cape Breton, a French fort of the 18th century; at Kings Landing, near Fredericton, N.B., a British settlement of the 19th century. Many historic homes have been preserved and are open to the public.

The Maritime region, with its 1.7 million people, is a microcosm of Canadian pluralism. The nation's first North American colony was established at Annapolis Royal (originally Port Royal) and the French-speaking Acadians who settled there are today scattered throughout the three provinces, still tenacious of their language and culture. Yankees, Loyalists, Blacks, Scots, Irish, English and "Dutch" (Germans) are also found, not to speak of the original Indian people, Micmacs and others. Every one of these ethnic groups has its own story. In a sense, then, to know Maritimers is to encounter their history.

Previous Pages
Kings Landing in winter, New Brunswick

HISTORIC SITES

NOVA SCOTIA

HALIFAX

HALIFAX, facing the Atlantic Ocean from the safety of Halifax Harbour, is on a peninsula with tidewater on three sides.

Province House, the legislative assembly for Nova Scotia, built in the early 1800s, is one of the finest examples of Georgian architecture in North America and the oldest such building still in use in Canada. It became the standard of other legislative buildings throughout the Maritimes. The first Responsible Government sat here in 1848.

Government House is the home of the lieutenant governor. It was built c. 1800 and reflects the use of all that was best in the architecture of the period. It is a Regency simplification of a Georgian exterior. The formal rooms are magnificent. The private residence, however, is not open to the public.

Citadel National Historic Park is the setting of the fourth citadel on this site. The first fort was a wooden palisade around Governor Edward Cornwallis's newly founded settlement in 1749. The present structure was started in 1828, took 30 years to build and was already obsolete by 1870. Happily, it has never been attacked in its long history. It was manned by British troops until 1906, when it was finally turned over to the Canadians. There are three museums within the park.

Old Town Clock, Citadel Park, has become synonymous with the city. The clock was donated by Prince Edward, Duke of Kent, who was stationed here from 1794 to 1800 and who made a fetish of punctuality. After leaving, he ordered a garrison clock made in London to be presented to the citizens of Halifax to ensure they would always know the time.

Historic Properties, on Halifax's waterfront, encompasses 12 buildings dating from the early and mid-19th century. Privateers Wharf is a stone building once used to house the booty captured by Nova Scotian privateers. Collins Bank is the former headquarters of Enos Collins, a local entrepreneur who was said to be the richest man in British North America when he died in 1871. The Halifax Banking Company opened offices in this building in 1825; in 1832 the company became the Bank of Nova Scotia, the first chartered bank in Canada. The Pickford Black building was built for Enos Collins in 1830. It has two-metre-thick stone foundations and outer walls of Acadian ironstone. The pitched slate roof and gabled brick firewalls make it one of the handsomest buildings on the wharf.

Prince's Lodge was built in 1794 as part of Prince Edward's residence. It is the only building of that complex still remaining. The prince spent time dallying with his Acadian mistress here. On the grounds there is a heart-shaped pool and paths spelling out her initials.

Prince of Wales Martello Tower was one of five towers erected by Prince Edward around Halifax. This is the only one still extant. The stone towers, built in 1796-97, were not used as defensive positions but for delaying action and were the prototype of a new system of coastal defence.

Governor's Quarters, Fort Louisbourg, Nova Scotia

Exterior Fort tower, Louisbourg, Nova Scotia

Old Citadel clock tower, Halifax, Nova Scotia

View of Louisbourg, 1731, Nova Scotia

St. Mary's Basilica was the first Roman Catholic church in Halifax and one of the oldest stone structures in Canada. Some parts date back to 1820. It has the tallest — 58 metres — polished granite spire in the world.

St. Paul's Anglican Church is the only remaining building from Halifax's founding in 1749. It was the first Protestant church in Canada and still has an elaborate royal pew. The cemetery is the oldest in the city and contains the graves of some of Halifax's founders. The church was originally outside the south palisade of the city.

York Redoubt was a defensive post when Major General James Ogilvie established a two-gun battery here in 1793. It was enlarged to eight guns by Prince Edward in 1796. A nine-metre-high martello tower was built here two years later. Its remains and the 19th-century gun emplacements can still be seen. From the 1860s to the end of the century, Halifax became one of the most important and heavily guarded naval bases in the British Empire.

HALIFAX AREA

LUNENBURG is one of North America's great fishing ports. The French settled here in the 17th century and by 1753 200 families, mainly from Switzerland and Germany, were ensconced. It was part of the English policy of placing loyal settlers in Acadia. St. Andrew's, built in 1828, has communion vessels given to it by George III. Zion Lutheran Church contains the chapel bell from Louisbourg. There is a monument commemorating the sack of Lunenburg by Boston privateers in 1782. The town is most famous for the *Bluenose*, launched in 1921, winner of four international schooner races. A replica, launched in 1963, was crafted in the same shipyard here.

MAHONE BAY was founded in the 1750s by New England settlers who were later joined by Loyalists. Three handsome 19th-century churches stand in a row at the edge of the bay. St. James' Anglican was completed in 1833, Trinity United in 1862, and St. John's Lutheran c. 1869. They are all traditional painted frame structures.

MOUNT UNIACKE: **Uniacke House** was the summer home of Richard John Uniacke, an Irish adventurer who became attorney general of Nova Scotia. He built this graceful colonial mansion between 1813 and 1815. The two-storey white wooden house with eight bedrooms once stood in the centre of a 2,025-hectare estate.

York Redoubt, Halifax, Nova Scotia

Sambro Lighthouse, sitting on a rocky island jutting into the Atlantic, is Canada's oldest operating lighthouse. The locally quarried stone structure is covered with wood. It stands 25 metres high, 43 metres above sea level and can be seen 27 km out to sea. The construction was financed by a tax on spirits and a lottery. It was once fortified and several abandoned cannon can still be seen.

☙

Shubenacadie Canal was started in 1826 but was abandoned until the 1860s. The route, 80 km of locks and canals, ran from Halifax to the Bay of Fundy. The canal has largely disappeared, but some of the locks remain.

☙

YARMOUTH: **Nonconformist House of Worship**, at Barrington, was built in 1765 by strict fundamentalist New England Nonconformists. It was originally called the Old Meeting House and is the oldest of its nature left in Canada. These meeting houses served as town halls and churches. In the 1830s it became a house of worship only. The clapboard structure is in the severe colonial style. A stove was installed in 1841 as concession to comfort. The architecture shows the influence of the carpenters who were shipbuilders as well.

Barrington District Courthouse is a typical Cape Cod structure and resembles the Old Meeting House in style. The two-storey Georgian building was built of local timber in 1841-43.

CAPE BRETON ISLAND

BADDECK: **Bell National Historic Park** was the summer home of Alexander Graham Bell. Bell, who spent nearly half his time here, doing much of his research at this location, first visited in 1885. Seven years later he established Beinn Bhreagh (Gaelic for beautiful mountain) on this headland overlooking the sea. He died here in 1922. There is a monument to the first airplane flight in the Commonwealth by Bell's associate, J. A. D. McCurdy, in the *Silver Dart* in 1909.

☙

IONA is named after the Hebridean island. This is where the Gaelic culture of the Highland Scots who settled in Nova Scotia is preserved. A pioneer museum and St. Columbia Church are located here.

☙

Battery at Fort Louisbourg, Nova Scotia

LOUISBOURG is the world's largest historical reconstruction. The original, commenced in 1719 by the French, wasn't completed until the 1740s. It was such a mammoth structure (3.2 km long), and so cripplingly expensive, that Louis XV said he expected to see its towers rising above the Atlantic. It was captured by the British in 1745, returned to the French by treaty and recaptured by the British in 1758. It was virtually destroyed in 1760. The reconstruction began in 1961.

The Garrison at Louisbourg housed as many as 5,000 men at one time and was the largest in North America. The restored buildings include the citadel guardhouse, the ice house, governor's carriage house and stables. The citadel itself boasts the largest collection of period furnishings outside France.

King's Bastion Barracks is a three-storey stone structure and was at one time the largest structure in the New World. It held the governor's residence, officers' quarters, soldiers' barracks, chapel and prison. This building is only one of four original bastions. It is ringed with walls 3.5 metres thick and nine metres high. At one time, Louisbourg had 148 cannons.

Louisbourg houses are made of wood and rough-cast masonry with roofs of bark, board, shingle or slate. Hôtel de la Marine is a waterfront tavern. Porte Frédéric's wooden gate was the main access to the harbour.

DIGBY AREA

ANNAPOLIS ROYAL has stately homes and its high street, St. George, is lined with fine historic buildings.

St. Paul's Cemetery, Halifax, Nova Scotia

View of the Fort and Port,
Town of Annapolis, Nova Scotia

McNamara House was a school in the 1790s; O'Dell Inn, now a museum, was a stagecoach stop in the mid-1800s. The Banks Residence is over 250 years old. Delancey House has foundations that date back to 1709. The original French dikes still hold back the tides of the Fundy.

Amberman House, Annapolis Royal area, is one of Nova Scotia's oldest houses, dating from c. 1730. Its salt-box style and the type of hinges used throughout were common in 18th-century New England. The nine-metre beams and pine panelling have been restored.

Fort Anne National Historic Park, Annapolis Royal, recalls the violent past of what is now a peaceful farming area. The first French settlement of the region began in 1605 and for the next century the French and English fiercely battled for possession. From 1710 to 1749, Annapolis Royal was the capital of Nova Scotia. A French bastion of 1702-08 and earthworks still exist. The site contains a reconstructed British officers' quarters from 1797. A powder magazine built in 1708 using limestone ballast is the oldest building in Canada outside Quebec.

PORT ROYAL: **Port Royal National Historic Park** began in 1605 as one of the first European settlements in North America. Samuel de Champlain was one of the founders. It was destroyed by British soldiers in 1613. The meticulously reconstructed fort duplicates Champlain's design. It forms a square around a courtyard in 16th-century farm style, fortified by a palisade. The furnishings are all reproductions from the 1600s. The enclosure houses the governor's residence, priest's house, chapel, guardroom, kitchen and bakery.

GRAND PRÉ AREA

Grand Pré National Historic Park, near Minas Basin at the head of Fundy Bay, preserves the memory of the 2,000 Acadians who were so cruelly expelled from these lands they had reclaimed from the sea in the 1670s. It was the largest settlement in Acadia and was completely destroyed by the British in 1704. The 1713 Treaty of Utrecht ceded Acadia to the British.

Judge Haliburton's House, Windsor,
Nova Scotia

Prince of Wales Tower, Halifax,
Nova Scotia

The French wrested it back again in 1747. The British began the expulsion in 1755. There is a reconstruction of a French-style chapel, which houses a historical collection. The statue of Evangeline by Philippe Hébert stands in front of it.

The Church of the Covenanters, built by the Loyalists in 1804, stands in the village. Evidence of Acadian industry in land reclamation is found throughout the area.

❧

WINDSOR: **Haliburton House** is the home of Judge Thomas Chandler Haliburton, who wrote the famous Sam Slick stories. He is considered the father of North American humorous writing. He began the house in 1835, just before his first stories were published. The house, now a museum, is furnished in the style of the 1830s and '40s.

OTHER HISTORIC SITES

MAITLAND AREA: **Kejimkujik Pictographs** are now part of a national park that protects Micmac Indian pictographs dating back to 1500. The Indians used hard rocks and beaver teeth to record battle and hunting scenes. There are sketches of animals, fish, canoes, even a paddlewheeler with the date 1849 on the stern. The park embraces some of the loveliest of the province's inland countryside.

❧

PICTOU: **Pictou County Courthouse** is completely intact. It was designed by architect David Sterling in 1856-57 and is a marvelous example of fine craftsmanship and elaborate ornamentation. The two-storey wood construction has massive cornices and the courtroom is embellished with stained-glass windows from England. The town includes the Micmac Museum, which is filled with objects from two Indian burial mounds that go back to the early 17th century.

Balmoral Grist Mill, Pictou area, was built in 1830 with stones weighing more than one tonne. They still grind grain every day, although the mill is now only a tourist attraction. The mill is completely restored and is one of the few water-driven mills in operation in the province.

Interior, Kings Landing,
New Brunswick

NEW BRUNSWICK

FREDERICTON

FREDERICTON's approach offers a sweeping view of the city along the Saint John River. Its most famous citizen, Lord Beaverbrook, left his imprint in many ways; his gifts to the town include a hockey arena, the Beaverbrook Art Gallery and the town's major theatre.

The Provincial Legislature was built in the early 1880s to replace the Old Province Hall, which was destroyed by fire. The Corinthian-inspired architecture has a central tower surmounted by a dome. The four fluted freestone columns on the Greek portico stand on pedestals of grey granite. The library has a rare, 1783 copy of the *Domesday Book*, originally written in 1086. The assembly chamber contains portraits of George III and Queen Charlotte.

Old Government House was the home of the colonial governor until 1892, when it became the official lieutenant governor's residence. The Georgian house was designed by architect John E. Woolford in 1828 to replace an earlier building destroyed by fire. It now houses the provincial Royal Canadian Mounted Police headquarters.

Old Burial Ground is the most historically important cemetery in New Brunswick. It has headstones from the 1787 to 1878 period, marking the graves of many Loyalists who founded the province.

Christ Church Cathedral, one of the finest examples of Gothic architecture in North America, was built between 1845 and 1853. It was deliberately modelled on a 13th-century English parish church, because in the 19th century it was felt that by following correct Gothic form the Anglican church could prove it was the true Catholic church.

The Guardhouse, 1828, part of the Military Compound (below), is restored to the 1820s period. It was occupied at that time by the famed Green Jackets Regiment. The Soldiers' barracks, 1826, housed the British infantry and depict the impossibly crowded conditions they lived in.

Kings Landing Mill, New Brunswick

The Military Compound contains officers' quarters built between 1839 and 1869. The older part has thicker walls of solid masonry and hand-hewn wood. The more recent section has thinner walls with milled wood. Stone arches, iron handrails and staircases are typical of the architecture of the Royal Engineers in the colonial period.

The University of New Brunswick was established in 1785 and is Canada's second-oldest institution of higher learning. The arts building, 1825-28, is the country's oldest university building still in use. The three-storey Georgian building was designed by John E. Woolford. The university is home of Canada's first astronomical observatory, 1851, and first engineering school, 1854.

York County Courthouse is the only courthouse in the Maritimes constructed to house both the courts and a market. It was one of the earliest brick buildings, 1855-7, and represented the trend away from wood and stone construction. The market was removed at a later date.

FREDERICTON AREA

GAGETOWN is home of the famous Loomcrofter Weavers, creators of tartans and other woven goods. They work in the oldest building on the Saint John River, a trading post erected c. 1760.

Tilley House, Gagetown, was the birthplace in 1818 of Sir Leonard Tilley, one of the Fathers of Confederation. The oldest part of the house dates from 1786, some rooms have been restored in early Victoriana and it is now the Queens County Museum.

Queens County Courthouse, Gagetown, is a lovely example of 1836 vernacular architecture. The one-and-a-half-storey edifice has a pediment supported by four large Tuscan columns, giving it a majestic templelike presence. ❧

PRINCE WILLIAM: **Kings Landing Historical Settlement** has 55 restored buildings, making it one of the most ambitious reconstructions in Canada. It conjures up the life that was lived along the Saint John River during the early and mid-19th century. It contains everything from log shanties to an inn with an eight-sided, 3.5-metre-high outhouse dubbed "the Taj Mahal of privies."

WOODSTOCK: The site of the world's longest covered bridge is at Hartland, near Woodstock. It is 390 metres long, has seven spans across the Saint John River and was erected in 1896.

Connell House, Woodstock, a two-storey wooden house, was erected in the 1820s by Charles Connell. He was the postmaster general of New Brunswick and most famous for substituting his own likeness for Queen Victoria's on an 1860 stamp issue. This is just one of several 19th-century houses in this pretty town.

MONCTON & AREA

MONCTON sits at the mouth of the Peticodiac River. A tidal bore as high as three-quarters of a metre goes up and down the river twice a day. Its other natural attraction is Magnetic Hill, which gives the impression that a car can coast up the hill — a powerful optical illusion.

Free Meeting House was constructed in 1821 by Baptist settlers from New England. A simple wooden building in the New England style, it has been used as a house of worship and first home for nearly every religious denomination in Moncton.

DORCHESTER: **Keillor House** is typical of the massive stone buildings in this town. The house is a nine-fireplace mansion built in 1813 in Regency style. It is now a museum.

Fort Beauséjour National Historic Park was built by the French in 1751 to defend their territories near the Bay of Fundy. It was captured by the British in 1755 and renamed Fort Cumberland, then abandoned in 1833. A pentagon-shaped outline formed by earthworks remains and archeologists have found remnants of many of the fort's original features.

ST. JOSEPH: **Survival of the Acadians National Historic Site** traces the history and culture of early Acadia through to the 19th and 20th centuries. The thematic exhibit is a good introduction for anyone interested in Acadian culture. The exhibit is housed in Monument Lefebvre, one of the original buildings in the College of St. Joseph, the first Acadian college in Canada.

Officers' Barracks, Fredericton,
New Brunswick

Old Government House, Fredericton, New Brunswick

Greenock Presbyterian Church, St. Andrews, New Brunswick

The Tower, Saint John,
New Brunswick

Old Courthouse staircase, Saint John, New Brunswick

Green Gables, Cavendish, Prince Edward Island

New Government House, Fredericton,
New Brunswick

OTHER HISTORIC SITES

Beaubears Island National Historic Park is on the Miramichi River, 80 km south of Bathurst. The French established a camp here in 1755 after the Acadians were expelled from Camp Beauséjour. Later in the century a shipyard was built on the island.

ST. ANDREWS: **St. Andrews Blockhouse** sits on a tip of land jutting into Passamaquoddy Bay. This blockhouse, now a national historic site, is one of three such structures paid for by the citizens of the town themselves. All were constructed during the War of 1812 to defend the town against American privateers. The survivor is 5.5 metres high and made with 30-cm timbers. The simple style of the blockhouse was an architectural response to the need for rapid construction.

Charlotte County Courthouse, St. Andrews, preserves the forms of 18th-century official British architecture. It was built by local craftsmen around 1840.

Greenock Presbyterian Church, St. Andrews, was built from local pine in 1825 by Captain Christopher Scott. An oak tree, painted bright green, is carved on the exterior. It was the emblem of Greenock, Scotland, Scott's birthplace. There are two hotels of note in the town: Shiretown Inn, 1881, one of Canada's oldest summer hotels; and the Algonquin, built in 1915.

Ministers Island Historic Site, St. Andrews area, holds the 202-hectare summer estate of William Van Horne, the first chief of Canadian Pacific Railway. The multiroofed, 28-room mansion was built in 1889.

Proposed Cathedral, Fredericton,
New Brunswick

Belfast, Prince Edward Island

Old Government House, Fredericton, New Brunswick

PRINCE EDWARD ISLAND

CHARLOTTETOWN

CHARLOTTETOWN nestles on the south shore of the island overlooking Hillsborough Bay on the Northumberland Strait. It was founded in 1764.

Province House is the three-storey, Georgian-style provincial legislative building built between 1843-47 entirely by Island craftsmen. The sandstone was imported from Nova Scotia. Delegates from Britain's four North American colonies met here in 1864 to discuss union. The original chairs and table used for that historic meeting are still used in the Confederation Chamber.

Government House is a modified colonial-style building with a Greek Revival portico. The white clapboard two-storey building was erected in 1834 and is home of the lieutenant governor.

Beaconsfield is a rich yellow three-storey mansion erected by shipbuilder James Peak. Today it is a museum housing ship models, 19th-century shipbuilding tools and nautical instruments.

St. Dunstan's Basilica is one of the Atlantic region's largest churches. The Gothic Revival-style building with twin spires is awe-inspiring. The interior is enhanced by a splendid altar and rose window.

Fort Amherst National Historic Park, Charlottetown area, now consists mainly of earthworks, but it has a long and honourable history. The traces of the fort rest at the entrance to the harbour across from the city itself. In 1720, Port la Joie became the capital of Île-Saint-Jean, as Prince Edward Island was known by the French who settled it. Three hundred settlers landed here that year. By 1758 it had become a British fort built after the French surrender. It fell into ruin by 1763, when the British decided to concentrate their efforts on the defense of Halifax.

CHARLOTTETOWN AREA

BELFAST: **St. John's Presbyterian Church** was built in 1823. The five-metre steeple is in the tradition of Sir Christopher Wren. Outside the church is a monument to the first Scottish settlers. The stones at the base were used as ballast in the ship that landed the settlers here in 1803.

❧

CAVENDISH: **Green Gables** is P.E.I.'s most famous export. Lucy Maud Montgomery set her famous Anne stories at this house, which belonged to her friends David and Margaret MacNeill. The house has been restored and is now a museum. Montgomery's grave is in the Cavendish cemetery.

❧

PORT HILL: **Green Park Provincial Historic Park** depicts shipbuilding, the island's main industry in the mid-19th century. The re-created shipyard has a smithy, sawpits, carpenter's shop and steam box for bending planks. There is also a keel and ribs from ships under construction. The Green Park mansion was built in 1865 as the home of shipbuilder James Yeo.

Lighthouse, Prince Edward Island

Province House, Charlottetown, Prince Edward Island

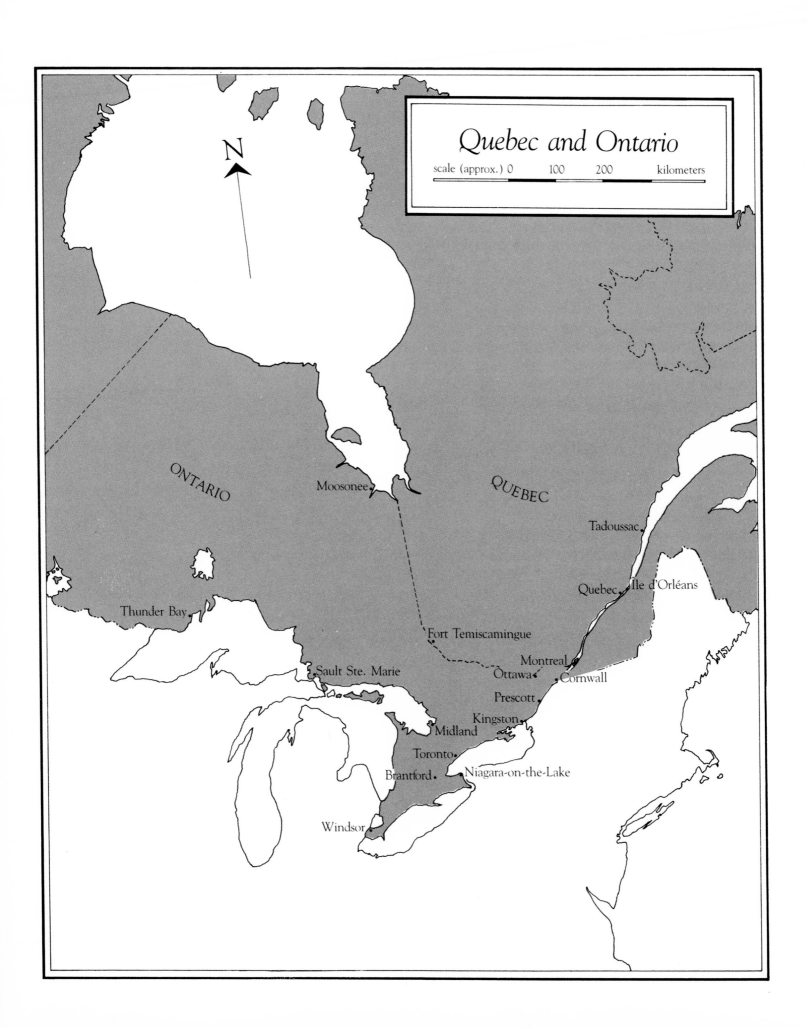

Quebec and Ontario

scale (approx.) 0   100   200   kilometers

N

ONTARIO

QUEBEC

Moosonee

Tadoussac

Quebec • Île d'Orléans

Thunder Bay

Fort Temiscamingue

Montreal

Sault Ste. Marie

Ottawa

Cornwall

Prescott

Kingston

Midland

Toronto

Brantford

Niagara-on-the-Lake

Windsor

QUEBEC

LA BELLE PROVINCE, formerly the colony of New France, is more than another province of Canada. For this unique nation within a nation, six and a half million strong, is the Other in Confederation, the alternative America, a redoubt of French-speaking, Catholic humanism in a continent of Protestant Anglo-Saxon positivism. The many churches, convents, seminaries and shrines of Quebec City and Montreal, the fine parish churches of the countryside, especially those of Île d'Orléans, pilgrimage shrines like Ste-Anne-de-Beaupré and St. Joseph's Oratory, testify to the profound religious devotion of French Canadians. At the Montreal Eucharistic Congress in 1910, Henri Bourassa told his countrymen, "Providence has willed that the principle group of this French and Catholic colonization should constitute in America a separate corner of the earth, where the social, religious and political situation most closely approximates to that which the Church teaches us to be the ideal state of society."

In effect, while French Canadians were at their prayers, Scots and English took over the fur trade and, in creating what was to be the nation of Canada in the vast hinterland of Montreal, created also the powerful metropolis which today is the second largest French-speaking city in the world. After the so-called Quiet Revolution of the 1950s and 1960s, a period of modernization, French Canadians saw their situation in a new light. The "English" had built their empire on the backs of French Canadians. Now it was the turn of French-speakers to be masters in their own house.

Reminders of Quebec's history are everywhere in this province. Quebec City strongly recalls New France and the Conquest. Old Montreal carries memories of the fur empire of the St. Lawrence; Trois-Rivières of the great days of the lumber industry, when *les raf'mans* (raftsmen) carried on the roistering tradition of the *voyageurs*. Even the long, narrow fields running back from the St. Lawrence are reminders of the early days, when *habitants* owed duty and obedience to their *seigneurs* and *curés*, and lived close together as though huddled against the threat of the Iroquois.

The Gaspé peninsula, where Jacques Cartier landed in 1534, is still deeply rural, not so much historic as timeless.

Overleaf
Quebec Citadel, Quebec City

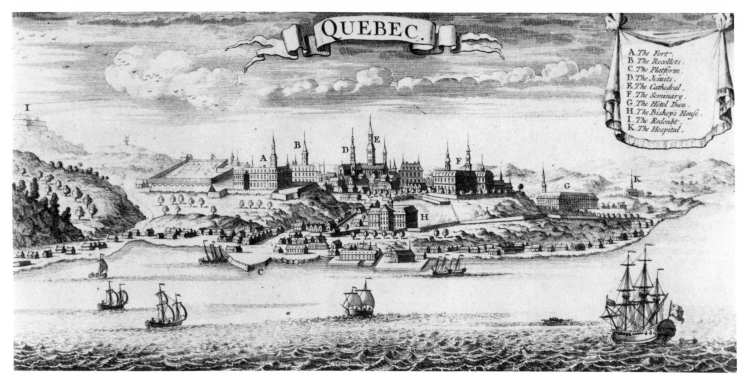

A. The Fort.
B. The Recollets.
C. The Platform.
D. The Jesuits.
E. The Cathedral.
F. The Seminary.
G. The Hotel Dieu.
H. The Bishop's House.
I. The Redoubt.
K. The Hospital.

View of Quebec City

Dufferin Terrace, Quebec City

HISTORIC SITES

QUEBEC CITY

QUEBEC CITY's site, chosen by Samuel de Champlain, is right on the St. Lawrence River, which he first explored in 1603. It was the hub of the fur trade at that time and its promontory afforded protection from the Iroquois, whom he had alienated when he sided with the Hurons. Founded in 1608, Quebec is the oldest city in Canada and the only walled city in North America. Several of the city gates, including the St-Louis, Kent and St-Jean, have been reconstructed.

The National Assembly, designed by Eugene Tache in an elegant Renaissance Revival style, was completed in 1886. The main building, flanked by corner towers, encloses a courtyard. The grey stone structure is covered with ivy and the recesses in the facade contain statues of 12 great men of Quebec. The assembly chamber has Charles Huot's fresco of historic scenes of Confederation.

Artillery Park National Historic Park covers about one-sixteenth of the area of Old Quebec City. It contains the Dauphine Redoubt, c. 1713, a massive building and one of the finest examples of French Regime military architecture. The New Barracks, 1749-54, and Captain's House, 1820, formerly the residence of the garrison commanding officer, are also in the park.

Basilica of Notre-Dame, Canada's oldest parish, was begun in 1647 on the foundation of Notre-Dame-de-Recouvrance, which Champlain built in 1633. The facade dates from 1843 and was designed by Thomas Baillargé. The south tower dates from 1689.

Battlefields Park is the site of the most decisive engagement in Canadian history: the Battle of the Plains of Abraham. Named after Abraham Martin, who grazed his cows outside Quebec's walls, this field was where General Wolfe defeated Montcalm in 1759 and captured the city. Both men died in the encounter.

Cartier-Brébeuf National Historic Park is the site where Jacques Cartier wintered in 1535. There is a replica of Cartier's flagship, *La Grande Hermine*. A 7.6-metre granite cross marks the spot where he raised a cross in 1535. The park is believed to be the place where Jean de Brébeuf built his house in 1626.

Château Frontenac, built in 1893-95, was the site of Château St-Louis, the French governor's residence. The grand red brick baronial edifice dominates the city's skyline and is one of the country's major hotels.

The Citadel, situated on the highest point of Cape Diamond, has been fortified since 1608, when Champlain built earthworks to protect his trading post. The British erected most of the present structure between 1823-32. There are two buildings from the French regime: Cape Redoubt, 1693 (the oldest military building in Quebec), and the powder magazine, 1750. The latter is now a museum.

City Hall is a five-storey building, built in 1895 on the site of a Jesuit College, 1635, and closed by the British in 1760. There is a statue of Louis Hébert, Quebec's first colonist, who arrived in 1617.

Dufferin Terrace was begun by Lord Dufferin. The boardwalk, with fanciful Victorian gazebos, overlooks the

Plains of Abraham, Quebec City

QUEBEC CITY AREA

BEAUPORT was the first settled parish on the Beaupré coast. It was founded in 1634 and is one of Canada's oldest communities. Aimé Marcoux House has parts that were built in 1655; the Girardin House is 300 years old.

❧

DESCHAMBAULT has at least one-third of its houses dating back more than a century. The English seized the town and burned down three houses in 1759. The Delisle House was rebuilt in 1764.

St-Joseph de Deschambault Church, Deschambault, was designed by architect Thomas Baillargé in 1834 and built in 1838. It is a classic twin-towered parish church and the only one still extant. The beautiful interior woodwork and sacred vessels were fashioned by famous Quebec artisans.

The rectory was built in 1735 and, along with the church, is an historic monument.

❧

ÎLE D'ORLÉANS is so important that the whole island has been declared an historic site. Churches and farms date from 200 to 300 years ago. It was named by Jacques Cartier for the Duc d'Orléans, son of Francis I. Roberval landed here in 1542, Champlain in 1608. It was first settled in 1648, and by 1712 there were five prosperous parishes on the island. Those parish churches indicate how central the church was to Quebec village life.

Wolfe and Montcalm Monument, Quebec City

Battle of The Plains of Abraham, 1759, Quebec City

Manoir Mauvide-Genest was an estate that once covered half of Île d'Orléans. When it was built in 1734, it was the largest in Quebec. The simple rectangular structure is, like most Quebec houses, without gables, wings or projections. It has rubble walls with cut stone dressing and a hip roof.

Ste-Famille Church is the most famous of the five churches. It was built in 1743 and is unusual because of its three bell towers. The west facade has five niches filled with gold-painted figures. The interior ornamentation is by the Baillargés. Among the French Regime houses in Ste-Famille parish: Ovide Morency, Andre Morency and Ulric Drouin. A huge stone windmill nearby is the last on the island.

Old Fortifications, Quebec City

Ste-Famille, Île d'Orléans

Place Royale, Quebec City

Château Frontenac, Quebec City

Moulin, Île d'Orléans

St-François Church, built in 1734, was requisitioned by the British as a hospital during the attack on Quebec in 1759. The pulpit, 1845, was carved by Louis-Xavier Leprohon; the vault and cornice, 1832-40, by Thomas Berlinguet; and the baptismal font, 1854, by Olivier Sanson.

St-Laurent Parish contains a four-storey stone water mill, now a restaurant, built c. 1635. The Gendreau House, pre-1759, has unusual architectural features for the island: a pointed red roof with two rows of dormers.

St-Pierre Church, in an early Norman style, was built from 1717-20. It has an open hall with a wooden elliptical vaulted ceiling. The stone walls are lined with wood-decorated Corinthian pilasters. The steep roof supports a wooden belfry.

✤

LAUZON: **Fort Lévis I** is the only survivor of three forts built in Lauzon in the 1860s to defend Quebec against American invasion. This restored, pentagon-shaped structure includes casemates, caponieres, ditches, tunnels, barracks and a powder house.

✤

Maison Montmorency was built in 1782 by Sir Frederick Haldimand, then governor general. It overlooks the spectacular 83.5-metre Montmorency Falls (30 metres higher than Niagara). From 1791-94 it was occupied by the Duke of Kent when he commanded the 7th Royal Fusiliers. One hundred years later it became a hotel. In 1954 it was acquired by Dominican Fathers.

Parish Church of Notre-Dame, 1820, Montreal

Overleaf
Worker's houses, Val Jalbert

MONTREAL & AREA

MONTREAL was the second city in Canada and is the second largest French-speaking city in the world. It is a city of bars (more than anywhere else in North America) and churches (550, almost as many as Rome). Its origins were as the Indian village of Hochelaga. In 1535, Jacques Cartier named the island in the St. Lawrence Mont Royal, for its 220-metre-high mountain.

Bonsecours Market, built of cut stone, became the temporary Parliament building for Canada after the legislative building was burned down during the riots of 1848. Until 1878 it served as the city hall. Its life as a market has been continuous since 1878. Its architecture is in complete harmony with the surrounding buildings.

Cartier House was the home of George-Etienne Cartier when he was practising law in the 1840s. He was one of the Fathers of Confederation. The three-storey stone residence was built in 1840s.

Château de Ramezay, built in 1705 by Claude de Ramezay when he was governor of Montreal, was the seat of government until his death in 1724. Benjamin Franklin dined here in 1775, when it was the headquarters of the invading American army. It is typical of the urban design of that period: an unbroken oblong with thick rubble walls projecting past the roof lines.

Congregation of Notre-Dame contains Centre Marguerite Bourgeoys, now a museum. The two stone towers to the east are remains of a fort where she and her disciples taught in the late 1600s.

Elgin House, the residence of Lord Elgin, was built by the Honourable James Monk, an early chief justice of Montreal. Lord Elgin, who served as governor general of Canada from 1847 to 1854, used this as his Montreal home during his tenure. It is attached to the Convent of Ville Marie and is constructed in an early Victorian style. During Elgin's stay here he refurbished it extensively and his monogram can be seen on many of the carvings and mouldings.

Grand Seminaire de Montréal started life as a fort built by the Sulpician Fathers in 1694. Two stone towers of the original building remain today. They are among the oldest structures in Montreal.

Hôtel de Ville is an ornate example of French Renaissance architecture. The city hall was modelled after the one in Paris and was built in 1926.

Joseph Papineau House, Montreal

Notre-Dame-de-Bonsecours, Montreal

Sulpician Brothers Convent, Quebec City

Notre-Dame Church, Montreal

St. Louis Gate, Quebec City

CHAMBLY has a number of fine old houses: St-Hubert, 1760; Maigneault House; Lareau House, 1775; and the Salaberry Manor, which is of Georgian design, unusual amid the more typical French Regime vernacular style of the town.

Fort Chambly National Historic Park was the first fort built by the French to protect the approaches to Montreal in 1665. The fort changed hands many times during the 17th and 18th centuries. It was originally built of logs; in 1709 the massive stone fortifications that still stand were begun. It was abandoned in 1851, but restorations were begun in 1882. Three walls have been rebuilt; the interior includes four bastions, the remains of storerooms and living quarters.

Couteau-du-Lac National Historic Park is located at the junction of the Delisle and St. Lawrence rivers. It contains remains of the canal and a British military post that protected the area during the War of 1812. A replica of the octagonal blockhouse has been erected. The canal, built in 1779-80, was the first in North America with locks.

ÎLE-AUX-NOIX: **Fort Lennox National Historic Park** is one of Canada's best examples of early-19th-century British military architecture. In 1759 this site was fortified by the French, then captured a year later by the British, who destroyed the fort. In 1775 Americans occupied this location. The stone garrison buildings date from the 1820s. Earthworks rise from a moat 18 metres wide and three metres deep. There is a renovated guardhouse, officers' quarters, canteen, barracks and commissariat.

Prince of Wales Terrace, classic stone-faced row housing, was built by Sir George Simpson, governor of the Hudson's Bay Company in 1860. It is a fine example of the terraces that were once so common in western Europe and North America.

Simon Fraser House was built in 1798. The two-storey stone house, now restored, was the residence of a North West Company partner (no relation to the explorer). He built it on the western tip of the island so that he could be the first to see fur-laden canoes coming down the Ottawa River.

Sulpician Seminary, built in 1685, is the oldest building in Montreal. The Clock, 1710, is one of Canada's oldest public clocks.

Le Moyne House, Longueuil

Interior of Notre-Dame Church, Montreal

Cartier's Ship, *La Grande Hermine*, Quebec City

Simon Fraser's House, Ste. Anne de Bellevue

Doors of Hotel de Ville, Montreal

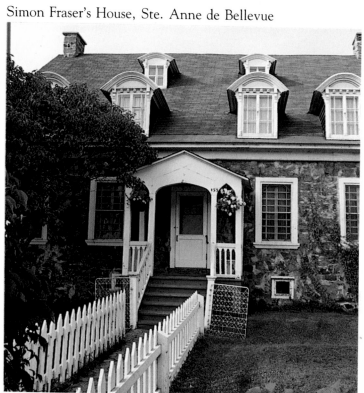

Fort Chambly, Montreal

LACHINE: **Lachine Manor**, 1670, one of Canada's oldest buildings, is now a museum. Many of the stone structures in Lachine are early 19th century. The Lachine Canal was built from 1821 to 1825 to bypass the rapids outside Montreal. Five hundred men dug a channel 14.5 metres wide with seven locks. It is still in use today.

LONGUEUIL: **Musée Charles Le Moyne** celebrates the founder of the town. Le Moyne built a fort in 1685 and this is a replica of that building, which was designed to protect the settlement from Iroquois raids. The museum displays books, charts and the effects of the Le Moyne family. It exemplifies the French Regime style of domestic architecture.

POINT CHARLES: **Ferme St-Gabriel** was originally a wooden farmhouse that burned and was replaced with this stone house in 1698. In 1668, Sister Bourgeoys bought the farm for her order. The rectangular building with .6-metre-thick rubble walls has been altered little since 1698 except for low wings at each end that were added from 1726-28.

ST-EUSTACHE: **St-Eustache Church** is where the fiercest battle of 1837 took place. Two hundred and fifty *patriotes* under Jean Olivier Chenon barricaded themselves against 2,000 British troops. The damaged church was rebuilt in the 1840s, but part of the facade and apse are original.

Ste-Anne Church, Tadoussac

Quebec from The Citadel

TROIS-RIVIÈRES: Les Forges du St-Maurice National Historic Site lasted as an ironworks until 1883. The first horseshoe nails were produced here in 1730. By 1741 the forges were the most important industry in New France. Now it is a series of ruins, including a 12-metre brick chimney and foundations of the Grand-Maison, 1737.

OTHER HISTORIC SITES

Fort Temiscamingue National Historic Site, Lake Temiscamingue, was a response by the French to the English forts built around James Bay in 1668. By 1790 the fort was in the hands of the North West Company and in 1821 it passed to the Hudson's Bay Company. It was finally abandoned in 1901. A few stone fireplaces and a cemetery are all that remain.

❧

ÎLE AUX COUDRES is a living miniature of 18th-century New France. Cartier first landed here in 1535 and the first mass on Canadian soil was celebrated the same day, September 7. The windmills, huge stone towers six to nine metres high, were used not only for grinding corn but as forts during Indian raids. Historic buildings include two chapels, several houses and the Desgagnés water- and windmills.

❧

ST-JEAN-PORT-JOLI is the wood-carving capital of Quebec. Most of the wood carving in the parish church, 1779, was done by such luminaries as the Baillargés, Perrault, Charron and Levasseur. The town serves as a link between Quebec's original wood-carving industry, established by Bishop Laval at St-Joachim, and its present-day revival here.

❧

TADOUSSAC, at the mouth of the Saguenay River, has the Pierre Chauvin House, a reconstruction of the first European structure on Canada's mainland. It was a fortified house built in 1660. Eglise Ste-Anne, 1747, is the oldest surviving chapel in North America. The bell, made in France in 1647, rests in a square 15-metre spire.

❧

VAL JALBERT has been a ghost town since 1927, after the closing of the local pulp mill. There are 63 buildings still intact, including a row of workers' houses. The latter are being restored.

❧

Overleaf
Elgin House, Montreal

The Waterfront at Kingston

ONTARIO

Loyalist refugees began settling in Ontario in 1783, clearing and cultivating land along the north shore of Lake Ontario and in the Niagara Peninsula. The cities of Kingston, Cornwall and Belleville date from this time. Other settlers poured in, drawn by the good land, and over the next two centuries Ontario became the richest, most populous Canadian province. It has a population (close to nine million) and economy roughly the size of Sweden's.

There are two capital cities in the province: Toronto, the provincial capital, and Ottawa, seat of the federal government.

Founded as the town of York by lieutenant governor John Graves Simcoe in 1793, Toronto was incorporated as a city in 1834. Ottawa was chosen as capital of the new dominion in 1867 by no less a personage than Queen Victoria.

In eastern Ontario, Kingston rapidly became the most important seaport on the lake. In the 1830s and '40s the British fortified the place, building the powerful Fort Henry and a series of martello towers to discourage Americans from a second round of the War of 1812, and perhaps also to overawe Canadians themselves. In the same period the Rideau Canal was built to connect Ottawa with the lake. Mighty public works of this kind helped to employ swarms of Irish and other immigrants who had little but their muscle to sell.

Southwest Ontario was largely settled through the efforts of an Irish aristocrat, Colonel Thomas Talbot, fourth son of a Talbot de Malahide. This reclusive, eccentric gentleman had the reputation of a tyrant, at least among the people he called "damned cold water-drinking Methodists" and their descendants. The colonel liked his bottle of claret and had no love for "impertinent democrats." Yet it was thanks to his driving force that roads were built, forests were cleared and the city of London, among others, rose in the backwoods.

Irish, English, Scots, Yankees, Germans and Dutch were among the pioneering stock of Ontario. The Irish brought their songs and factional fights and, as elsewhere, a talent for politics. The English and Scots brought sober industry and Protestant capitalism — pray on the knees Sundays, on other days prey on the neighbours. The Yankees brought frontier skills; the Germans a certain earnestness and a sound knowledge of music and beer.

Some immigrants brought books, and in places like Lakefield, Brockville, Cobourg and Niagara-on-the-Lake as well as Toronto there was a

Overleaf
Fort at Sainte-Marie among the Hurons, Midland

social hierarchy led by a cultivated gentry. The Grange, now part of the Art Gallery of Ontario, is a reflection of that life, the stately home of Goldwin Smith, a scholar and a gentleman.

But most Ontarians lived more simply, as may be seen in such reconstructions as Upper Canada Village at Morrisburg and Black Creek Pioneer Village, Toronto. The province abounds with museums, large and small, reflecting the lives and occupations of Ontarians in time past. And of the others who came before them: the fur barons of the North West Company who wined and dined in Fort William at Thunder Bay; the Mohawks at Brantford; and the Jesuit martyrs at Midland.

View of Fort George from Old Fort Niagara, Niagara-on-the-Lake

HISTORIC SITES

TORONTO

TORONTO, a port city on Lake Ontario, was built on gently rolling hills. It was designed by Governor Simcoe's engineers, who laid it out in a grid pattern that can still be discerned in the oldest part of the city.

Queen's Park, the Provincial Legislature, built from 1886-92, was designed by R.A. Waite, chairman of the architectural selection committee. He rejected all other designs, contending that he could do a better job himself. The Romanesque-style structure with Celtic and Indo-Germanic carvings as embellishment is constructed of sandstone and has a slate roof.

Black Creek Pioneer Village stands on the site of pioneer Daniel Stone's farm. Five log buildings are original; 25 other buildings were moved from elsewhere. They date from 1816 to 1844 and the village looks much as it did in those days.

Casa Loma, North America's largest castle and, some say, biggest folly, was constructed by Sir Henry Pellatt from 1911 to 1914. There are 98 rooms, plus hidden passageways and secret staircases. This reproduction of a medieval English castle has a 244-metre tunnel leading to one extremely handsome building: the stables.

Campbell House was built in 1822. William Campbell was chief justice of the court of Upper Canada, and speaker of the legislature in the 1820s. The restored Georgian mansion, typical of Family Compact dwellings of the period, was moved to its present site by the Law Society in 1972.

Fort York was established in 1793 to protect the new capital of Upper Canada. Destroyed in 1813 it was rebuilt and used as the garrison headquarters until 1841. There are eight original structures within the earthworks.

Gibraltar Point Lighthouse, built in 1808, is one of Toronto's oldest landmarks and the oldest lighthouse on the Great Lakes. This hexagonal structure is built of Queenston limestone.

Gibson House was built by David Gibson, a follower of William Lyon Mackenzie. His earlier home was destroyed in the 1837 Rebellion and Gibson fled to the United States. When he returned in 1849, he constructed this red brick Georgian home, which was completed in 1851 and has been restored to that era.

The Grange, attached to the Art Gallery of Ontario, has been restored to its former glory as a gentleman's home of the 1835 period. It was the centre of social and political life for the Family Compact society when it was built in 1817 by D'Arcy Boulton.

Fort York, Toronto

Interior, Osgoode Hall Library, Toronto

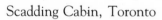

Scadding Cabin, Toronto

Parliament Buildings, Ottawa

Mackenzie House, Toronto

Fort Henry, Kingston

Parliament Buildings, Ottawa

Merrick Tavern, 1830, and Merrick Sawmill, 1848, are also extant.

MORRISBURG: **Upper Canada Village** Cornwall area, is a giant combination of relocation, reconstruction and restoration of building and life between 1784 and 1867. Forty pioneer buildings have been moved here that span that era. Glengarry County Home, c. 1840, is characteristic of the fine Georgian-style structures built by the Loyalists along the St. Lawrence, all with classical proportions.

ST. ANDREWS WEST, Cornwall area, has the oldest remaining stone church in Ontario. St. Andrew's Church was built in 1801 and is now a parish hall. It was the first church built by Roman Catholic Scots Highlanders in Upper Canada. Simon Fraser's grave is in the cemetery opposite new St. Andrew's Church, 1860.

KINGSTON & AREA

KINGSTON, one of the loveliest and most humane cities in the country, was founded in 1673 by the French gov-

ernor general of New France, Louis de Buade de Frontenac. The stockade built by Frontenac was replaced with stone bastions by La Salle, appointed the fort's commander by Frontenac. La Salle also named the fort Frontenac, which it remained until 1758, when it fell to the British. In 1784, a number of United Empire Loyalists settled here, renaming it Kingston. During the War of 1812, Kingston was a military base for the British. From 1841-44, it was the capital of Canada.

Bellevue House, built c. 1840 by a retired grocer, was leased to Sir John A. Macdonald as a country house for his wife, Isabella, from 1848 to 1849. It was built in the style of a Tuscan villa of stuccoed brick; ornamental fretwork adorns the eaves.

Kingston City Hall was never used for the national legislative assembly, as was hoped when the building was started in 1841: the capital was moved to Montreal before the building was completed. The stunningly handsome structure in the Classical style has soaring Doric columns and is con-

Previous Pages

St. Raphaels, Lancaster

Death of Brock, Battle of Queenston Heights

Brock's Monument, Queenston Heights

structed of the local limestone that gives many of Kingston's buildings their unique character.

Fort Henry is a gigantic construction. It was built on Point Henry between 1832 and 1836 to protect the southern terminus of the newly completed Rideau Canal. The fort has been restored and demonstrates 19th-century military life. The famous Fort Henry Guard performs drills during the summer months. Nearby Royal Military College was Canada's first military academy.

Frontenac County Courthouse was designed by Edward Horsey and built from 1855 to '58. He loosely mixed Italianate and Classical details in this imposing building. When a fire in 1865 destroyed the dome, it was redesigned by another architect to give it an even greater emphasis.

Grimason House-Royal Tavern was owned by Eliza Grimason, a life-long friend of Sir John A. Macdonald. After Macdonald became prime minister, the inn became his unofficial political headquarters.

Murney Redoubt, one of the last martello towers built in Canada, is a magnificent example of stonemasonry. It was one of four erected in this area during the 1840s. Another, Fort Frederick Tower, on the grounds of RMC, is also open to the public.

St. George's Cathedral began as a garrison church in 1825 and grew to become an Anglican cathedral when the new church was built in 1882.

Tête de Pont Barracks. Parts of the foundation walls of the old Fort Frontenac are visible near the parade square. The buildings in the compound are now occupied by the National Defence College.

AMHERSTVIEW: **The White House** is a superb example of the homes affluent Loyalists built in this area. This one was built by William Fairfield Sr. in 1793. Five generations of his family have lived here.

BATH: **Fairfield House** was built by William Fairfield Jr. in 1796. It is colonial architecture at its most brilliant. Bath was the seat of Upper Canada's first court. Another notable example of Loyalist architecture is the home of Jeptha Hawley, built in the 1780s. Willowbank Forge has 2,700 historic iron pieces on display.

BROCKVILLE shelters one of the oldest public buildings in Ontario. The courthouse was built in 1842 on a grand scale using the Palladian style. The detailing is very sophisticated. It faces onto a public green, each of the four corners of which is occupied by a Victorian church.

Frontenac County Courthouse, Kingston

Previous Pages
Bellevue House, Kingston

Frederick B Taylor   38/100

Government House, Ottawa

PICTON is filled with the treasures of Prince Edward, Canada's only island county. The courthouse, 1832-34, is the oldest Greek Revival building in Ontario. Old St. Mary Magdalene's Church, completed in 1827, is a red brick Gothic edifice that is now a museum. West Lake Boarding School, a brick Georgian farmhouse built in 1835, was Canada's first Quaker seminary.

NIAGARA-ON-THE-LAKE & AREA

NIAGARA-ON-THE-LAKE became Upper Canada's first capital in 1792. Most of the homes in this lovely town were built after the War of 1812 in the neo-classical Regency style, replacing the Georgian-style houses destroyed by retreating Americans during the war. The exquisitely restored homes are privately owned; a few are open to the public one day each June.

Butler's Barracks National Historic Site housed Butler's Rangers, who fought on the Loyalist side during the Revolutionary War. The barracks were erected in 1778, but burned in 1800. The current barracks date from 1815. Only four of the original 20 structures remain.

The Courthouse, built in the Palladian style in 1846-47, illustrates a transition to larger, more sophisticated buildings outside the major centres. William Thomas was the architect of this pleasing building.

Joseph Brant, Chief of The Six Nations Indians, Brantford

defenses, which surround a masonry tower.

McFarland House, built in 1800 of handmade bricks in the Georgian style, is now a museum. The furnishings are from the 1820-30 period.

St. Andrew's Presbyterian Church is a very fine Greek Revival design with an imposing classical portico. It was built in 1831.

St. Mark's Church, first built in 1804, was used as a hospital by the British and a barracks by the Americans during the War of 1812. It was rebuilt in 1822.

❧

FORT ERIE: **Old Fort Erie** was first built in 1764. The first and second constructions were destroyed by ice and flooding. The third, 1805-08, was captured by the Americans in 1814. They destroyed and then abandoned it. Re-created in 1939, the fort has a dry moat, drawbridge, bastions and guns typical of the early 19th century.

❧

QUEENSTON: **Brock Monument** is a second attempt to celebrate Major General Sir Isaac Brock. The first was blown up by supporters of the 1837 Rebellion. The second, built in 1856, commemorates Brock's troops' victory over the Americans in 1812. He was killed by a sniper's bullet during the battle and is buried beneath the 56-metre monument.

Fort George National Historic Park is situated on high ground on the Niagara River, guarding the river and the town. The buildings of the original fort were started in 1796 and this was the principal British fort on the Niagara frontier in the War of 1812. At this reconstruction the layout consists of six earthen bastions connected by cedar picketing. Living quarters and other buildings of timber are re-creations of structures of the 1796-1813 period.

Fort Mississauga was built to replace Fort George after it was razed during the War of 1812. Rubble and brick from the ruins of the town were used in its construction in 1813-14. It has unusual star-shaped earthworks and

Laura Secord House is now a restored one-and-a-half-storey museum. In 1813, Secord overheard American officers planning a rout of the British forces. She walked nearly 32 km through the woods, driving a cow before her, and gave the warning that saved the British from surprise attack.

❧

Overleaf
Dundurn Castle, Hamilton

OTTAWA AREA

OTTAWA stands on the Ottawa River overlooking the Rideau Canal. At first it was called Bytown, after Colonel John By, who came here in 1826 with the Royal Engineers to start the building of the canal. The name was changed in 1855, and Queen Victoria declared it as the new capital of Canada in 1857. It was dubbed the "Westminster of the Wilderness."

The Houses of Parliament, begun in 1859 and completed in 1876, burned down in 1916 and were restored in the Gothic style. This was a deliberate choice. Officials wanted the buildings to be as unlike the Capitol in Washington, D.C., as possible, and to be similar to the parliament buildings in London. There are three buildings: the Centre Block, bristling with gargoyles and dominated by the 91-metre Peace Tower, holds the House of Commons

Penetanguishene, Midland

Penetanguishene, Midland

PENETANGUISHENE.

MIDLAND.

Fort Erie

and the Senate Chamber. Behind the Centre Block is the Parliamentary Library, the only part of the buildings to survive the 1916 fire. The East Block contains the governor general's, prime minister's and Privy Council's offices. The West Block is filled with other government offices.

Government House, built c. 1838, serves as the residence of the governor general of Canada. It is a three-storey limestone edifice on a 35-hectare estate. The style is Scottish manorial.

Bytown Museum, Ottawa's oldest building, was erected in 1827 by Colonel By. The three-storey stone commissariat is filled with relics and documents relating to the construction of the Rideau Canal and the history of Bytown.

Laurier House was built in 1878. In 1897, Sir Wilfrid Laurier purchased the house and lived here when he was prime minister and until his death in 1919. It was bequeathed to William Lyon Mackenzie King, who lived here from 1923 to 1950.

OTHER HISTORIC SITES

KEENE: **Hopewell Mounds** are 2,000 years old. One, the serpent mound, is 1.5 metres high and 58 metres long. The purpose of these mounds, built by the Hopewellians, is unknown. Nearby is Lang Century Village, a re-creation of life in early Upper Canada.

❧

MIDLAND: **Sainte-Marie among the Hurons** was established in 1639 in the heart of Huronia by Jesuit missionaries who longed to have a Christian community as an example of civilized life. In 1649, it was burned to prevent its capture. Four Jesuits were martyred

Upper Canada Village, Morrisburg

Interior of the Fort, Sainte-Marie among the Hurons, Midland

The Blue Church, Prescott

ST. LAWRENCE HALL, KING STREET, TORONTO.

St. Lawrence Hall, Toronto

by the invading Iroquois. A reconstruction of the palisade and buildings now hums with life as it was then lived. There is an artificial waterway to allow canoes to be paddled inside the stockade from the Wye River. On the hill below stands the Martyrs' Shrine, the first in North America outside Mexico. The grave of one of the martyrs, Jean de Brébeuf, is at the Indian church.

Huron Indian Village, Midland, is a palisaded reconstruction of a 17th-century Indian village. The vaulted longhouse could shelter up to 20 families.

✔

MOOSONEE: **Moose Factory** built on an island on the Moose River in 1673, is Ontario's oldest fur-trading post and was the first English settlement in Ontario. The Moose Factory Museum Park has a restored log fort, powder magazine and a 1740s blacksmith shop (where pioneer bellows are still in operation). The island is also the home of Cree Indians. St. Thomas' Anglican Church, built in 1864 as a church for the Crees, has a moosehide altar cloth and hymnbooks in the Cree language.

✔

Fort William, Thunder Bay

Penetanguishene, Midland area, was established in 1813-14 as a naval base to protect British supply routes to Fort Michilimackinac on Lake Michigan. After the War of 1812, it became a shipbuilding centre. It was garrisoned until 1856. There is one surviving military building, the officers' quarters, which is now a museum. Other buildings, such as the guardhouse and sawpit, are reconstructions. There are skeleton hulls of two ships on the grounds. St. James-on-the-Lines garrison church, built in 1836-38, is still used.

❧

PETERBOROUGH AREA: **Peterborough Petroglyphs** comprise 300 figures carved into limestone. They were discovered in the early 1950s and date c. A.D. 1000 to 1500. The forms include animals, humans, mythic shapes and fertility symbols.

❧

PORT ELGIN: **Port Elgin Indian Village** is a reconstruction of a 600-year-old Indian village on its original site. Archeologists restored the site, guided by soil mouldings and other marks from wood that rotted away hundreds of years ago.

❧

PRESCOTT: **Blue Church** is the third wooden chapel on this site. It was built in 1845 in the midst of one of the oldest settled parts of the province. The grave of Barbara Heck, founder of Methodism in Upper Canada is here.

Fort Wellington National Historic Park, Prescott, has as its main attraction a three-storey blockhouse built in 1838. The fort was established during the War of 1812. It was from here that the gallant soldiers marched across the ice and captured the American fort at Ogdensburg, New York. The fort was used again during the 1837 Rebellion. The blockhouse is the largest in Canada. Other original features include the gigantic earthworks and a stone caponiere.

Battle of the Windmill National Historic Site, near Prescott. The battle for which this site is named took place over five days near Fort Wellington in 1838. Rebels and their American supporters landed in an attempt to capture the British fort, thus leaving Upper Canada vulnerable to invasion. They lost. In 1878, a beacon was mounted on the windmill and served as a lighthouse until the early 1920s. The windmill is now being restored.

❧

Casa Loma, Toronto

Militia encampment at Fort Wellington, Prescott

Sir William Campbell House, Toronto

THUNDER BAY: **Fort William** built in 1803 on the site of the old French portage route, was the chief inland post of the North West Company. It took 1,000 men years to build it. The reconstruction is 14 km upstream from the original portage site. There are 42 buildings. The Great Hall was for the dining and dancing pleasure of the company officers and traders. The walls are 4.5 metres high. The barns reflect the French building styles of the day. Jean Marie Boucher's Tavern is just outside the walls.

❧

WINDSOR AREA: **Fort Malden National Historic Park** on the Detroit River, was built in 1796 when the British evacuated Fort Detroit. General Brock led an attack on Detroit from here in 1812. It was burned by its British defenders in 1813; after their retreat, American troops occupied its ruins. Following the peace treaty, the British regained the site and built a smaller fort. During the 1837 Rebellion, Fort Malden was repaired and continued to be garrisoned until 1851. From 1859 to 1870, it was used as a lunatic asylum and then allowed to moulder. There are the remains of the bastions, a restored pensioner's cottage and an original 1820 barracks. A brick building from the asylum period contains exhibits.

❧

SAULT STE. MARIE AREA: **Fort St. Joseph National Historic Park** is located on the southwest tip of St. Joseph Island. In 1796, the British built the fort to counter the American presence at Fort Michilimackinac. It was the western headquarters of the British during the War of 1812. In 1814 it was burned by the Americans and only the stone bakehouse, powder magazine and a chimney remain. Archeological excavations reveal the outlines of palisades and the foundations of the blockhouse, guardhouse, two bakeries and traders' huts.

❧

Overleaf
Fort Wellington, Prescott
Barnum House, Grafton

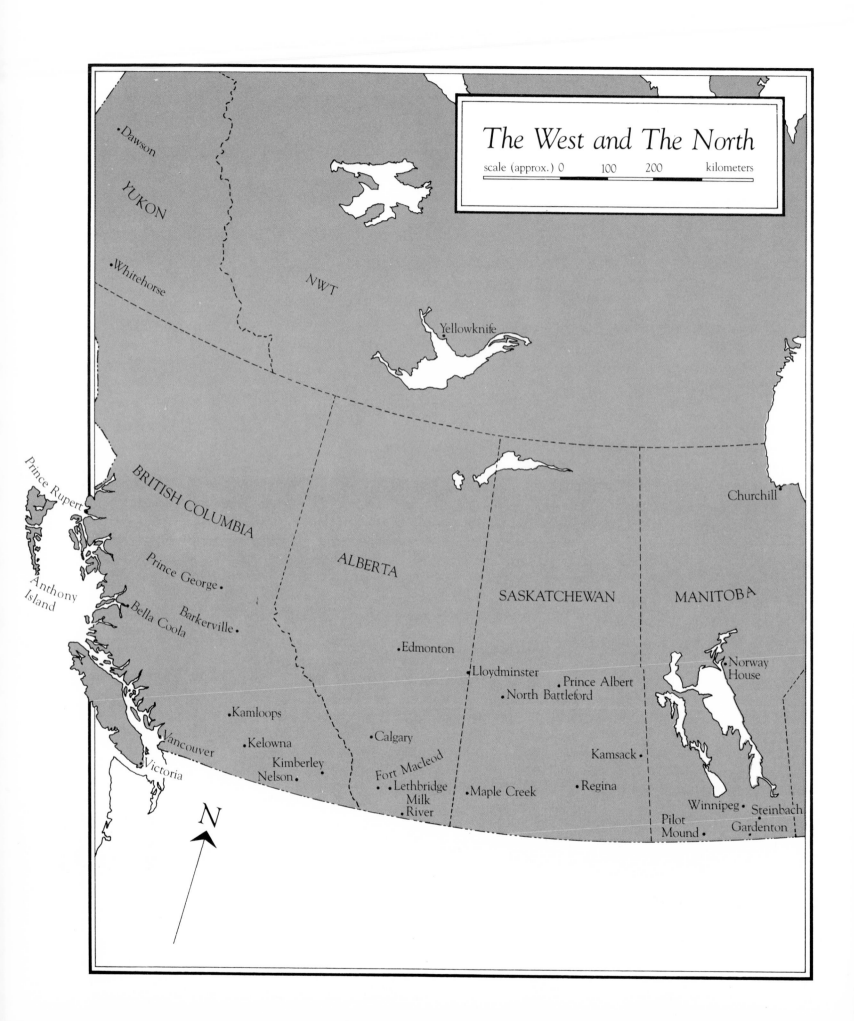

The West and The North

scale (approx.) 0   100   200   kilometers

Dawson

YUKON

Whitehorse

NWT

Yellowknife

Prince Rupert

Anthony
Island

BRITISH COLUMBIA

Churchill

Prince George

Bella Coola

Barkerville

ALBERTA

SASKATCHEWAN

MANITOBA

Edmonton

Lloydminster

Prince Albert

North Battleford

Norway
House

Kamloops

Vancouver

Kelowna

Calgary

Kamsack

Victoria

Kimberley
Nelson

Fort Macleod

Maple Creek

Regina

Lethbridge
Milk
River

Winnipeg

Steinbach

Pilot
Mound

Gardenton

N

THE PRAIRIES

IT WAS MORE THAN 200 YEARS after Henry Kelsey first came to the prairies near "the great and filthy lake of the Hurons" (Winnipeg) that homesteaders first arrived on the great plains. Lord Selkirk founded a settlement near the forks of the Red and Assiniboine rivers in 1812, where La Vérendrye had set up a trading post in 1738. The Red River settlement failed at first, thanks to harassment by fur traders and Métis. As late as 1849, Sir George Simpson was adamant that the region around the Red River was not suitable for settlement.

In time the settlement "took," acquiring its own miniature government and judiciary. In 1868-69, Métis resistance came to a head when Louis Riel declared a provisional government. The rebellion was crushed and in 1870 the province of Manitoba was created. Settlers flocked in with the new railway. The worst fears of the Métis were realized as they saw homesteads rising on their hunting grounds, and in 1885 they were again led in revolt by Louis Riel. There is little doubt that the man was demented, suffering from some kind of religious mania. Never the less, the Orangemen of Ontario wanted him hanged. French Canadians were enraged, but Prime Minister John A. Macdonald calculated that there were more votes in hanging than in reprieve. The execution of Riel left permanent bitterness between "English" Protestants and "French" Catholics not only in Manitoba, where it still festers, but across Canada.

Saskatchewan was made a province in 1905 and, with Manitoba, the region began to develop as the breadbasket of the world. Winnipeg grew rich on grain brokerage. And then, as the depression of the 1930s struck with catastrophic force, the whole area became poor overnight.

Cumberland House, Saskatchewan

Saulteaux Indians, Manitoba

To financial disaster, as world markets collapsed, nature added its own torments: in Saskatchewan rains failed, topsoil turned to dust and rust destroyed the wheat.

Winnipeg had already suffered from social conflict. The General Strike of 1919 had left bitterness in its wake. There had been anger and violence, almost outright class war. Jews and foreigners had stirred up the people, muttered the capitalists. In fact, the leading radicals had been cold-water Methodists.

Anger exploded again in 1935. In Regina, capital of Saskatchewan, police fought a pitched battle with 3,000 men from the work camps who were marching on Ottawa. This episode is not commemorated in Regina, perhaps because it does not reflect glory on the Royal Canadian Mounted Police, who have a training depot here. But Mountie heroes are remembered in the RCMP museum at the depot.

Away off to the north, just over the tree line, by Hudson Bay, is Churchill, once an important Hudson's Bay Company post and the site of Fort Prince of Wales. During World War II, Churchill became a summer grain port.

Previous Pages
Riel Grave, St. Boniface Cathedral, Manitoba

HISTORIC SITES

MANITOBA

WINNIPEG

WINNIPEG, situated at the confluence of the Red and Assiniboine rivers, is the capital of Manitoba and Canada's fifth-largest city. St. Boniface, a suburb, is the largest French-speaking community in the country outside Quebec.

Provincial Legislature was completed in 1919. This Classical Greek-style structure is made of Tyndall limestone quarried near the city. On top of the 73-metre dome perches the *Golden Boy*. The running youth holding a wheat sheaf was sculpted by Charles Gardet, who also created two bronze buffalo that flank the grand marble staircase.

Fort Garry Park contains one gate of the 1835 Hudson's Bay Company's Upper Fort Garry. A tablet commemorates three former forts on this site: Fort Rouge, 1738, Fort Gibraltar, 1804, and Fort Garry, 1821.

Grant's Mill, built by Cuthbert Grant in 1829, is believed to have been the first watermill west of the Great Lakes and the first one to generate hydro power in Manitoba. The original gristmill was constructed on Sturgeon Creek; a replica of the mill is now in the city.

Ross House was built between 1852 and 1854 by William Ross, son of the Hudson's Bay Company's chief factor. The log building became the first post office in the west.

St. Boniface Cathedral, burned in 1967, was rebuilt behind the facade of the previous building. This handsome Gothic structure occupies the site of Winnipeg's first church, built 1818; the yard contains the grave of Louis Riel.

St. Boniface Museum was built by the Grey Nuns in 1846. Originally a convent, orphanage, hospital and old people's home, it now is a museum containing settlers' belongings. Outside there are four grinding stones brought from Scotland and used by Louis Riel's father, who was a miller.

St. James Church, built in 1853, is the oldest log church in western Canada.

Seven Oaks House, the oldest still-habitable house in Manitoba, was constructed from 1851-53. The house was built entirely without nails because they were too expensive to import from England. The two-storey clapboard home was put up by John Inkster, a local merchant. It is now a museum with its original furnishings and some of Inkster's possessions.

Seven Oaks Massacre is commemorated by a 2.75-metre limestone column that marks the site where, in 1816, Métis led by Cuthbert Grant, a North

Lower Fort Garry, Red River, Manitoba

Lower Fort Garry — or Stone Fort — Red River.

Fort Walsh National Historical Park, Saskatchewan

Interior Lower Fort Garry, Manitoba

Lower Fort Garry, Manitoba

St. Michael's Ukrainian Orthodox Church,
Gardenton, Manitoba

Fort Prince of Wales,
Manitoba

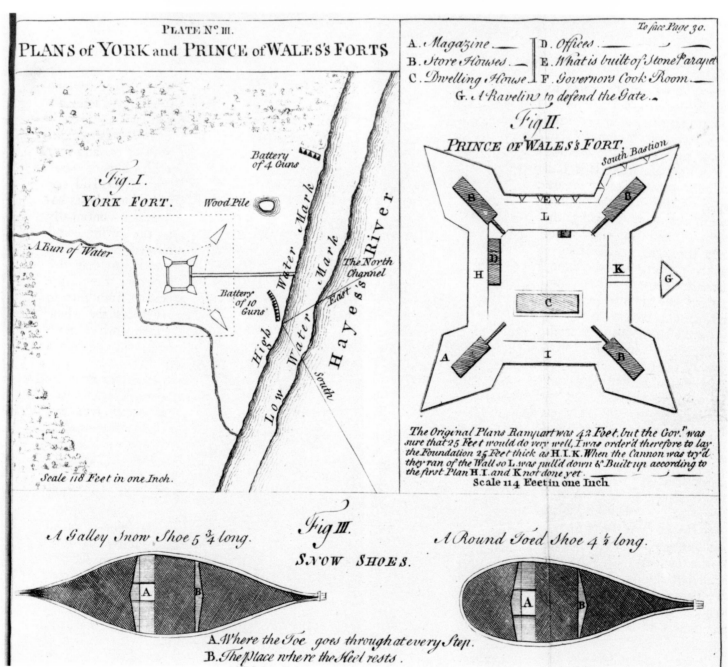

PLATE N.° III.

PLANS of YORK and PRINCE of WALES's FORTS

To face Page 30.

A. Magazine
B. Store Houses
C. Dwelling House
D. Offices
E. What is built of Stone Parapet
F. Governors Cook Room
G. A Ravelin to defend the Gate.

Fig. I.
YORK FORT.

Battery of 4 Guns

Wood Pile

A Run of Water

A Run of Water

Battery of 10 Guns

The North Channel

Water Mark
High Water Mark
Low Water Mark
East
South
Hayes's River

Scale 118 Feet in one Inch.

Fig II.
PRINCE OF WALES's FORT.

South Bastion

The Original Plans Rampart was 42 Feet, but the Gov.ʳ was sure that 25 Feet would do very well, I was order'd therefore to lay the Foundation 25 Feet thick as H. I. K. When the Cannon was try'd they ran of the Wall so L. was pull'd down & Built up according to the first Plan H. I. and K not done yet.
Scale 114 Feet in one Inch

Fig III.
SNOW SHOES.

A Galley Snow Shoe 5 ¾ long.

A Round Toed Shoe 4 ½ long.

A. Where the Toe goes through at every Step.
B. The Place where the Heel rests.

The Nunnery at Red River, Manitoba

Plans of York and Prince of Wales Forts, Manitoba

Overleaf
Fort Prince of Wales, Manitoba

West Company clerk, clashed with Governor Robert Semple, killing Semple and 20 Red River settlers.

WINNIPEG AREA

LOCKPORT: **St. Andrew's Lock** opened in 1910, is the only lock on the prairies. It bypassed the rapids on the Red River. St. Andrew's Anglican Church was built in the early 1800s and is the oldest stone church in western Canada. The rectory, 1853, is now a museum. The church has its original fixtures and buffalo-hide-covered kneelers. Red River House Museum, 1866, evokes 19th-century colonial life.

❧

PORTAGE LA PRAIRIE: **Fort la Reine** is a replica of a fort built by La Vérendrye in 1738. It was used as his headquarters during explorations of the prairies. The palisaded fort contains a log trading post. Also on the site are a log house, c. 1880, and a church, 1883.

❧

SELKIRK: **Lower Fort Garry National Historic Park** built in 1830, was the Hudson's Bay Company's headquarters until 1837. Thirteen reconstructed buildings are now on the site. The Big House, built by HBC Governor George Simpson for his bride, is a two-storey Regency cottage with a hip roof, dormer windows and wide verandas. It looks more like a gentleman's country residence than a company house. Fraser House, in the town of Selkirk, is typical of Red River settlers' dwellings in 1835.

OTHER HISTORIC SITES

CHURCHILL: **Fort Prince of Wales National Historic Park** is located at the mouth of the Churchill River. This Hudson's Bay Company post was begun in 1731 and was not completed until 1771. In 1775, Samuel Hearne became governor. Hearne surrendered the giant stone fort to the Fench in 1782 without a shot being fired. They sacked and destroyed it in two days. The walls of the fort, nine to 12 metres thick at the base, have been partially restored, as have several other buildings.

❧

GARDENTON: **St. Michael's Ukrainian Orthodox Church** built in Manitoba's first Ukrainian settlement, is the oldest Orthodox church in Canada. The log building was ready in 1899 and wooden siding was added the following year. There are hand-carved candelabra and icons from Russia on display.

❧

Old Fort Garry (demolished 1882), Winnipeg, Manitoba

Norway House, north end of Lake Winnipeg, was built in 1826 as a Hudson's Bay Company post. It has the original warehouse, gateway and powder magazine. The mission of James Evans was established in 1840 outside the Norway House post at Rossville. Evans was the inventor of a phonetic alphabet for the Cree Indians.

PILOT MOUND contains archeological evidence of a 1,000-year-old civilization. A plaque records the 1908 excavation of an Indian burial mound. There is a suggestion that the mound was later used by Indians as a place for ceremonial dances and a gathering place for buffalo hunters.

Nellie McClung Cabin, La Rivière, near Pilot Mound, housed this legendary feminist while she was teaching school here in the 1890s. It was built of logs in 1878 and has been restored to the period during which she lived here. It is at the Archibald Historical Museum in La Rivière.

STEINBACH: **Mennonite Village Museum** reconstruction of a Mennonite town built in 1874. It includes a farmhouse with such distinctive middle-European features as a connecting barn. A windmill, cheese factory, church-schoolhouse and thatched-roof log cabin are also part of the village. A modern building contains Mennonite documents, books dating from the 16th century and domestic items.

York Factory National Historic Site, operated for 275 years as a trading post. The Hudson's Bay Company first established a post in 1682, but this site dates from 1788. The depot building, 1830, is York Factory's major feature. The site can be reached only by chartered plane or canoe.

The Entrance to Government House, Fort Garry, Manitoba

St. Boniface Cathedral, Red River, Manitoba

SASKATCHEWAN

REGINA

REGINA has been a capital city since 1882. It is located in the southeastern part of the province on the South Saskatchewan River. The name Regina was chosen in honour of Queen Victoria.

The Provincial Legislature was built between 1908-12. The impressive domed structure has 34 types of marble in its interior. The library displays the table used by the Fathers of Confederation at the Quebec Conference of 1864.

Diefenbaker Homestead is also on the same grounds of Wascana Centre as the legislative buildings. John Diefenbaker lived in this three-room frame home as a boy. It was built in 1906 and moved from Borden, Saskatchewan, in 1967.

REGINA AREA

ABERNETHY: **Motherwell Homestead** is one of the first homes indicative of the province's prosperity and a distinct move away from prairie vernacular architecture. It was built in 1897 by Richard Motherwell, later a member of Mackenzie King's cabinet. It is one of the few remaining cut stone prairie buildings. The restored 10-room house is of a basic Georgian design with Italianate features popular in the mid-19th century. It has been restored to the 1920s period.

❧

Fort Qu'Appelle, built in 1864, was originally a Hudson's Bay Company post. It was a militia base during the Northwest Rebellion of 1885. A small log and mud cabin, 1864, is part of what is now a museum. A cairn marks the site where Indians surrendered 195,000 square km of land in 1874.

NORTH BATTLEFORD & AREA

NORTH BATTLEFORD: **Battleford National Historic Park** was established in 1876 as a NWMP post. It was the capital of the Northwest Territories until 1883. In 1885, during the Northwest Rebellion, it became a refuge for settlers fearing an Indian attack. Poundmaker surrendered here after the Métis' defeat at Batoche. Five of the original buildings remain and a stockade has been reconstructed on the site. The pioneer village includes old buildings and homes moved here for preservation.

❧

CUT KNIFE: **Poundmaker's Grave** sits in stark isolation on the Cree reserve that bears his name. He was accused of fomenting war during the Rebellion of 1885 and, though he protested his innocence, was sentenced to prison

Cannington Manor, Manor, Saskatchewan

Fort Carlton, Saskatchewan

Peter Verigin's House, Veregin, Saskatchewan

Poundmaker's Grave, Saskatchewan

Fort Garry, Manitoba

Fort Walsh, Cypress Mountains, Saskatchewan

Fort Carlton, Saskatchewan

An English Settlement in the North-West

The Mill

The Village of Cannington

Mr Hanson's

Beckton Bros (in course of construction)

Sketches in Cannington Manor,
Saskatchewan

Overleaf
Outbuilding, Cannington Manor,
Saskatchewan

for a year. He died shortly after his release.

Fort Carlton, near North Battleford is a reconstruction of a Hudson's Bay Company post built in 1810. It was headquarters of the Northern Council in 1821, when the HBC and the North West Company merged. It was the departure point for the Canadian force that marched to Duck Lake in the first engagement of the 1885 Rebellion.

PRINCE ALBERT & AREA

PRINCE ALBERT is filled with the history of the Great Rebellion of 1885. It has a Presbyterian church built in 1866 by Reverend James Nisbet. The little log church was one of the first in Saskatchewan and is now a museum. The graves of the NWMP killed during the rebellion are in the cemetery of St. Mary's Church, 1874-76. A cairn on the north shore of the Saskatchewan River marks the site where Peter Pond established a fur trading post in 1776. The city also has the Dominion Land Office, 1873, and Emmanuel College, 1881, an ornate Victorian structure.

Batoche National Historic Site commemorates the decisive battle of the 1885 Rebellion. Batoche was the capital of the Métis' provisional government, and it was here that the roughly 160 Indians and Métis led by Gabriel Dumont met the 700-strong force of Major General Frederick Middleton. Though the Métis had constructed an intricate system of trenches and rifle pits, some of which remain, they were unable to withstand the withering fire of the Gatling guns Middleton's troops employed. The rectory of the Church of Saint-Antoine-de-Padoue, 1884, still bears scars of the battle.

Duck Lake Battlefield has a monument to the first battle of the Northwest Rebellion. The Métis, anxious to secure their land rights, rose up in 1885 under the leadership of Louis Riel. A North West Mounted Police force marched from Fort Carlton to Duck Lake, where the Métis and Indians under Gabriel Dumont defeated the NWMP.

OTHER HISTORIC SITES

VICTOR: **St. Victor Petroglyphs** are etched in an 18-metre-high sandstone outcropping. Neither the people who did them nor when they were done is known. The 40 symbols depict hand-, face- and footprints and apparently had

Sioux Indian Camp, Saskatchewan

religious significance. A restored log house, 1889, holds the McGillis Museum, furnished in late-19th-century fashion.

❧

KAMSACK: **St. Andrew's Anglican Church** built in 1885 by Saulteaux Indians, is one of the oldest in the province. There are six pews of hand-hewn boards, a handmade baptismal font and mats woven from bulrushes. The belfry bell was cast in 1888.

❧

MANOR: **Cannington Manor** was a colony established by English aristocrats in the late 19th century. Built in 1882, it was an attempt to re-create the amenities of English country life. All Saints Anglican Church has been restored; the three-storey Hewlett House, home of James Humphrys, who designed most of Cannington Manor's buildings, is open to the public. Beckton Mansion, 16 km east, was once the centre of the settlement's sporting life. It is a now-derelict 26-room stone mansion.

❧

CUMBERLAND HOUSE was named for Prince Rupert, Duke of Cumberland. it was established in 1774 by Samuel Hearne and is the oldest settlement in Saskatchewan. The remaining structures are white painted wood. The hulk of the HBC steamer *Northcote*, used to carry troops against the Métis at Batoche, is still here.

❧

MAPLE CREEK contains a North West Mounted Police cemetery, which includes the grave of Louis Lavallie, a famous scout and interpreter. "A" Division of the NWMP moved here after abandoning Fort Walsh in 1883. Frontier Village, seven km south, has several buildings from the area, including a log church, house and school, all of which date from 1894 to 1915.

❧

Fort Walsh National Historic Park was the site of a fort established in 1875, two years after 20 Indians had been killed nearby by white traders. The fort was used to maintain peace when the Sioux fled to Canada in 1876, after the Battle of Little Big Horn. It was abandoned in 1883. In 1942, the Royal Canadian Mounted Police built a horse ranch here, constructing the buildings in the same style as the original fort.

Cypress Hills Massacre site, where the Indians were murdered in 1873, is marked by Farwell's Trading Post, reconstructed in Fort Walsh National Historic Park. It displays trading items used in the 19th century, including "bad whiskey."

❧

The first Cathedral of Saskatchewan, Prince Albert, Saskatchewan

The Fight at Duck Lake, 1885, Saskatchewan

VEREGIN: **Doukhobor Prayerhouse** was built in 1917 by Peter Vasilovich Verigin, the leader of the sect. The Doukhobors began arriving here in 1899 and the white clapboard prayerhouse is still used for services.

Wood Mountain Post is an 1874 North West Mounted Police station. A barracks and mess hall have been reconstructed. In 1876, a detachment was stationed here to police the Sioux after they fled north following their victory at Little Big Horn under the leadership of Sitting Bull.

Battleford Barracks, Saskatchewan

Churches at Batoche, Saskatchewan

Motherwell Homestead, Abernethy, Manitoba

Indians greeting the Governor at Red River, Manitoba

ALBERTA & THE NORTH

In 1795 THE HUDSON'S BAY COMPANY established Edmonton House in its drive to exploit the furs of the Athabaska region. More than a century later, when rumours of Klondike gold brought a rush of prospectors to the post, smart traders supplied and equipped them for their arduous trek north. Edmonton is still a gateway to the north, and still outfits people heading toward the Arctic. When the province of Alberta was created in 1905, Edmonton became its capital.

From Edmonton the early bush pilots pioneered the art of flying over wilderness where magnetic compasses went crazy and lubricants had to be heated with a blowtorch before engines would start.

Today Edmonton and Calgary are rich and thriving cities. They have grown on oil, and Alberta has grown with them. In many ways the province has become a kind of northern Texas, with a cowboy mystique, a streak of old-fashioned religion and a flamboyant social style.

The oil business began in 1914 with a lucky strike in the Turner Valley. It boomed with the Leduc discovery in 1947. Along with oil there was natural gas.

The cowboy cult is strongest in Calgary, centre of the ranching country, especially during the famous stampede. The original Fort Calgary, though, was not a cattle market but a police station. Here the North West (Royal Canadian) Mounted Police set up a post in 1875 as part of their campaign against whiskey-runners and hoodlums from south of the border. Historic sites in Alberta lean heavily toward the early days of the RCMP and the fur trade, church missions and pioneers.

At Fort Whoop-Up, near modern Lethbridge, a number of late-19th-century outrages led to the formation of the Mounties. Whiskey traders from Montana were invading Canada with all the violence and criminality of their own Wild West. Fort Whoop-Up was a post where traders made Indians drunk, then cheated and abused them. In 1870 rival tribesmen had become so inflamed that they fought a pitched battle, in which at least 250 died. The North West Mounted Police were formed to see that the Canadian west would not be an imitation of the American frontier. They were given the scarlet coats, and imbued with the spirit of British cavalry. Luckily, they proved more intelligent than their Old-Country models. Here there would be no Charge of the Light Brigade; no Custer's Last Stand either, for that matter. Their firmness, discipline and tact kept the Queen's peace throughout the west and north.

Fort Macleod, Alberta

Today the RCMP are a presence in every Canadian province and across the Northwest Territories. So, after more than three centuries, is the Hudson's Bay Company, now a department-store chain. The capital and largest centre of that immense waste is Yellowknife, whose 10,000 souls can discover history by talking with neighbours. Yellowknife was founded away back in 1935.

Previous Pages
Fort Edmonton, Alberta

HISTORIC SITES

ALBERTA
EDMONTON

EDMONTON sprawls on either side of the North Saskatchewan River, a glittering city that belies its origin as a Hudson's Bay post in 1795. Since 1905 it has been capital of the province.

The Legislative Building, a high-domed structure, contains marble from Italy, Quebec and Pennsylvania. The interior features lavish carved oak and mahogany doors.

Old Government House is a 1913 sandstone mansion that was once the lieutenant governor's residence. It has been restored as a provincial reception centre, and is part of the provincial museum and archives.

Fort Edmonton Park is a reconstruction of the original fort. Workmen used the same tools employed in the 18th century. Palisades and bastions enclose an Indian trading house, married men's quarters, a bachelor's hall and the chief factor's Big House. An Indian village, lumber and gristmills are included in the park as well.

Fort Edmonton, 1880, Alberta

George McDougall Church, an 1871 wooden structure, is the oldest in the city. It is now a museum dedicated to the missionary work begun in 1862 by Reverend George McDougall.

Rutherford House is a brick building built in 1911 by the first premier of Alberta, A.C. Rutherford. It has been restored to the period.

John Walter Historic Site is an 1874 log house built by Walter, who was a boat builder. It was the first home outside the walls of Fort Edmonton. In 1886 he built a more elaborate and comfortable home, which has been restored.

EDMONTON AREA

Fort Victoria was established as a mission in 1862 by the Methodists. The Hudson's Bay Company built a fort here in 1864, which has been replicated and is now a museum. The chief factor's house is a one-and-a-half-storey, mud plastered and white-washed log structure. It is the oldest house in the province on its original foundations. Other buildings include a general store and the Pakan Church, 1863.

❖

MARKERVILLE was the reception centre for 50 Icelandic colonists in 1888. They established two towns. Stephannson House, built in 1889, was added to in 1893. The house reflects the life of early Alberta farmers. On the site there is Hola school, a Lutheran church, a creamery and Johnson's store.

❖

ST. ALBERT was founded in 1861 by Reverend Albert Lacombe from Montreal. He was a missionary to the Indians and mediated between the Cree and Blackfoot, who were traditional enemies. His missions dot

the prairies and tales of his goodness are legion. He wrote a Blackfoot dictionary and a Cree prayer book. The log chapel here was built in 1861, enlarged in 1864 and designated Alberta's first cathedral in 1868. Since 1929 it has been preserved in the brick building of the Father Lacombe Museum.

CALGARY & AREA

CALGARY is Canada's highest city, 1,048 metres above sea level. With the Rocky Mountains as a staggering backdrop, the city sits comfortably in the valley of the Bow and Elbow rivers.

Fort Calgary, a North West Mounted Police post built in 1875, has only its foundations remaining. On the site is Deane House, an 1876 log cabin, the oldest in Calgary. It was the home of one of the fort's early commanding officers.

Heritage Park is an historic village depicting life in the early Canadian west. The Wainright Hotel is a reconstruction of the showplace of prairie architecture, destroyed in 1929. It has a two-storey outhouse. The pine log opera house, 1896, general store, 1905, and an example of the sod houses commonly used by settlers when no wood was available are part of the pioneer exhibit.

❧

DRUMHELLER: **Dinosaur Provincial Park** is the world's richest burial ground of prehistoric creatures. Bones date back 70 million years. Also located here is the cabin of John Ware, a slave from South Carolina who became a cowboy and started one of Alberta's first ranches in the late 1880s.

❧

View of Rocky Mountain House, 1873, Alberta

Fort Macleod, originally located on an island in the Oldman River, has been reconstructed on the edge of the town. It was named for North West Mounted Police Assistant Commissioner Colonel James Macleod, who spent the first winter here in 1874-75. Buildings include a museum with Indian relics, early NWMP weapons and uniforms, a law office, blacksmith's shop and chapel.

Head Smashed-In Buffalo Jump near Fort Macleod is an 18-metre vertical drop used by Indians as a way of killing buffalo. Drive lines of piled stones start 11 km from the cliff. At the base is a 10.5-metre layer of bones.

❧

LETHBRIDGE: **Fort Whoop-Up Indian Battle Park** marks the site of the last great Indian battle in Canada, in 1870. Inside the park there is a replica of the fort with its original cannon. Traders from here were responsible for the 1873 Cypress Hills Massacre, which prompted the formation of the North West Mounted Police.

❧

Previous Pages
Fort Whoop-Up, Alberta

Fort Macleod, c. 1875, Alberta

Fort Macleod, Alberta

Interior Father Lacombe's Chapel, St. Albert, Alberta

Spirit Houses, Champagne, Yukon

Fort Macleod, Alberta

S.S. *Klondike*, Whitehorse, Yukon

Fort Edmonton, Alberta

MORLEY: **McDougall Memorial Church** the first Protestant church in southern Alberta, was built for the Stony Indians by Methodist missionaries George and John McDougall in 1876. Twice a year services featuring a choir singing in Cree are held.

OTHER HISTORIC SITES

LLOYDMINSTER: **Barr Colony** on the Alberta-Saskatchewan border, was the result of a remarkable public-relations campaign in England. One thousand colonists arrived here in 1903, having been recruited by Reverend Isaac Moses Barr. Barr was dismissed in Saskatoon and the settlers chose Reverend George Exton Lloyd as their leader. Lloyd, after whom Lloydminster is named, later became the first Anglican bishop of Saskatchewan. The Barr Colony Museum contains St. John's Minster, a 1904 log church, a log school and replicas of homes.

Fort Pitt, Lloydminster area, was a major Hudson's Bay Company post from 1829 to 1885. One of its NWMP defenders was Inspector Francis Dickens (son of Charles Dickens). One building has been reconstructed.

☙

MILK RIVER: **Writing-on-Stone Provincial Park** contains dozens of Indian rock carvings that were drawn on the sandstone walls of a coulee over a 300-year period. Several were done by Sioux warriors after the 1876 Little Big Horn victory.

☙

Rocky Mountain House was established by the North West Company in 1799. David Thompson used this post as a base for his explorations of the Rocky Mountains. The post remained open as a trading centre for Plains Indians until abandoned in 1861. Only two stone chimneys dating from that era still exist; the other structures here are replicas.

THE NORTH:
THE YUKON AND THE NORTHWEST TERRITORIES

DAWSON CITY

DAWSON CITY, Yukon, had grown to a city of 30,000 by 1899, three years after gold had been discovered. By 1900 it was already starting to decline. The commercial centre had houses, hotels and shops that varied wildly in architectural styles — from simple to floridly ornate.

Bonanza Hotel, a three-storey log hotel built in 1898, is Dawson's oldest building.

Courthouse and Administrative Building, 1899, replaced a hastily built log court when a show of substantial government was necessary to keep the gold miners under control. Both wooden buildings were planned by Thomas Fuller and have classical motifs.

Encampment of Blackfoot Indians, Alberta

Mission of St. Albert, 1877, N.W.T.

Robert Service Cabin was the home of the bank teller who became a famous poet. He lived and wrote here from 1909-12. The cabin has been restored and daily readings by his "ghost" are one of the Klondike International Park's main attractions.

Bonanza Creek, Dawson area, still has Gold Dredge Number 4, the largest of its kind in North America. It worked Bonanza Creek for many years. A cairn marks the spot where the nugget that started the boom was found on August 17, 1896.

Diamond Tooth Gertie's was a gold-rush gambling hall, a place for cancan girls and just one of the many dance-halls and gambling saloons that spread along the wooden streets of the town. It now operates as a casino during the summer months.

WHITEHORSE

WHITEHORSE, Yukon, lies at the end of the Trail of '98, followed by thousands of prospectors dreaming of instant riches. An old log church, 1900, served as the cathedral of the Yukon until 1959, when Christ Church was built. Sam McGee's cabin is here, moved from its original site at Lake Laberge, where it was when Robert Service wrote *The Cremation of Sam McGee*. At the Indian Burial Ground many of the graves are covered with spirit houses to protect the dead.

S.S. Klondike National Historic Site, Whitehorse, commemorates S.S. *Klondike*, a sternwheeler that was the last of what was once the Yukon's main form of transportation. From the late 1860s to the 1950s, 250 of these vessels plied the Yukon River from Whitehorse to Dawson. The S.S. *Klondike*, built in 1937, made its last run in 1955.

Heritage Park, Calgary, Alberta

McDougall Church, Morley, Alberta

View of New Westminster, c. 1880

BRITISH COLUMBIA

Historic places in the Pacific province are not hard to find. Often they are marked by plaques inscribed with some of the most superheated prose ever cast in bronze. At points on the Fraser Highway, the visitor, alerted by one of these plaques, may look into the canyon to see the river raging below, then read the story in which the torrent is always "the mighty Fraser." Nevertheless, it is with awe that one confronts the fact that Simon Fraser, and many a trader after him, descended that river to the sea.

British Columbia was discovered by Europeans from two directions at once. Alexander Mackenzie crossed the Rockies and reached the Pacific Ocean at Dean Channel in 1793. The Spanish Captain Quadra and the British Captain Vancouver arrived in Nootka Sound in 1791, pursuing rival claims.

Vancouver's claim prevailed. He had been an able seaman under Captain James Cook on his voyage of 1771, and a midshipman under him when Cook sailed into Nootka Sound in 1778. (Cook, for his part, had been an able seaman at the fall of Quebec in 1759.) Vancouver surveyed the coast northward from Juan de Fuca Strait, sailing into Burrard Inlet in 1792, where the great city bearing his name now stands.

In 1846 the Hudson's Bay Company established its Pacific headquarters at Fort Victoria on Vancouver Island. It became the capital of British Columbia when the former colony entered Confederation as a province in 1871.

The first passenger train arrived in Vancouver in 1887. The city had grown up around Coal Harbor, Burrard Inlet, and was at first called Granville. It was nicknamed Gastown after a hotel keeper called Gassy Jack. Sir William Van Horne of the Canadian Pacific Railway renamed the new town Vancouver.

The region came alive with the Fraser gold rush of 1858 and the Cariboo gold rush of the early 1860s. With the arrival of the railroad, Vancouver began to develop as a significant seaport. Grain from the prairies arrived for shipment to the Orient; tea from the Orient, with silks, china and other luxury goods, arrived for transport by rail to eastern Canada. The province began to build its economy on lumber, mining and fishing.

Artisan Shop, Fort Langley

Indian tribes of the Pacific coast — Haida, Kwakiutl and others — still create magnificent works of religious and heraldic art. These are on display in several museums and cultural centres, and for those who have time to visit the Queen Charlotte Islands decaying totem poles may be seen in their original sites.

View of Esquimalt Harbour, 1880

HISTORIC SITES

VICTORIA

VICTORIA rests gently on the southern tip of Vancouver Island. It is the most elegant and the most British of all Canadian cities — in sharp contrast with its past. It began as Fort Victoria, a fur trading post, in 1843 and began to grow in the 1850s, when it became a provisioning base for the thousands of prospectors heading to the Fraser gold fields. It became the capital in 1868.

Provincial Legislative Buildings were completed in time for Queen Victoria's Diamond Jubilee. They replace the 1859 pagodalike structures that had formerly been on the site. They were designed by Frances Rattenbury using only material from British Columbia, with a grey stone facade and slate roof. The main building is topped with a dome surmounted by a statue of Captain George Vancouver, who claimed these territories for the British in 1792.

Chinese School's turned-up eaves give it the flavour to blend in with Victoria's Chinatown. It was built in 1909. The Chinese who moved here in the gold rush of 1858 wanted to ensure that their children retained their cultural heritage and so built the first school in 1885.

Craigdarroch Castle was started by Robert Dunsmuir in 1856, the fulfillment of a romantic promise to build a castle for his bride to induce her to leave Scotland, which she did in 1851. He died before it was completed, but his widow moved in. The castle has Elizabethan chimneys, a steep pink roof, grey stone walls and masses of stained glass.

Craigflower Manor National Historic Site was built in 1856 by the Hudson's Bay Company, which was entrusted with colonizing the city with British immigrants. The company bought four farms to supply Fort Victoria with fruit and vegetables. The two-storey clapboard building is in the colonial style and built to resemble the birthplace of Kenneth MacKenzie, the farm's first manager. It is now a museum.

Craigflower School is the oldest standing school west of the Great Lakes. It was built in 1855 and is now a museum of pioneer life.

Dominion Customs House was erected as a reminder that the city was now part of Canada in 1876, ending Victoria's free port status. The solid red brick building was designed by T.S. Scott and has the mansard-style roof typical of many government buildings of the period.

Emily Carr House is a two-storey frame house where the famous painter was born on December 13, 1871. She spent part of her childhood here and wrote about it in *The House of Small*. The house has been restored, and some of her letters and drawings are on display.

Fisgard Lighthouse marks the mouth of the Esquimalt Harbour. It was the first lighthouse on Canada's Pacific coast. The 1859 structure is built of bricks, which were shipped around Cape Horn from England. The keeper's living quarters were gutted by fire in 1957. The tower and living quarters have since been restored to their 1873 appearance.

Cottonwood House, Quesnel

Craigflower Manor, Victoria

Old Hastings Mill, Vancouver

Point Ellice House, Victoria

Oldest church, Yale

View of New Westminster

Fort Rodd Hill was established when a Russian gunboat entered the Strait of Juan de Fuca. Victorians, in a panic at the thought that the Russians might invade, constructed the upper and lower batteries in 1895. It became the most extensive artillery fortification on the west coast of Canada and was operational until 1956. The fortifications are intact.

Hatley Castle was built by James Dunsmuir, who became premier, then lieutenant governor. The house, built of local stone in 1908, has 50 rooms and creates an imposing presence with its 25-metre turret. In 1937, it became Royal Roads Military College.

The Maritime Museum was originally built as the Victoria Courthouse in 1887, and was the city's first concrete structure. The building, with its unusual Romanesque towers and Italianate windows, rests on the site of Fort Victoria. The museum has a superb collection of scale model boats plus the 11-metre *Tilikum*, a dugout canoe modified to a three-masted schooner that sailed around the Cape of Good Hope at the turn of the century.

Point Ellice House, the home of Peter O'Reilly, the colony's first gold commissioner, was built c. 1861. It has been restored to the period and has a large collection of Victorian furnishings.

St. Ann's Academy was built in 1858 by the Sisters of St. Ann, who taught Hudson's Bay Company officials' and employees' children. The core area of the academy was built in 1871 and the wings were added later. It's a solid brick four-storey building with ornate dual stairway. St. Andrew's Church, incorporated in 1882, is at the rear.

VICTORIA AREA

Alert Bay, Cormorant Island, reflects the best of west coast Indian architecture. The community house has hand-hewn roof beams, supporting totem poles and stylized heads designed on the walls. The cemetery has some of the most graceful and important totems on the coast. The memorial pole for Mungo Martin is significant. It was he who kept the art of totem carving alive among the Kwakiutl Indians.

※

Nanaimo Bastion still has two original cannon from the fort and blockhouse. It was built in 1853 to shelter the British brought by the Hudson's Bay Company to dig coal. Displays include trade goods from the 1852-62 period and other items related to HBC history.

KAMLOOPS & AREA

KAMLOOPS: **Fort Kamloops**, a log Hudson's Bay trading post built in 1821, has been dismantled and reassembled in the Kamloops Museum. A replica of the fort can be found in Riverside park.

The Coaling Station, 1859, Nanaimo

Blockhouse, Hudson's Bay Company Fort

Ashcroft Manor was the name given the house built by two Cambridge brothers, Clement and Henry Cornwall, in 1862. They lived the life of English gentlemen and rode to hounds — after coyote. It became a well-known stop on the Cariboo Trail. The Cornwalls' house and log church still exist.

❧

Quilchena Hotel, south of Kamloops, was built by speculators in 1908. They believed a branch line of the Canadian Pacific Railway was coming through. When it took a different route, this elegant white elephant was left alone in the wilderness. The three-storey Victorian building is still in operation today.

❧

KELOWNA: **Father Pandosy Mission** was the first white settlement in the Okanagan Valley. It was built in 1858 by Father Charles Pandosy, an Oblate priest. He was the first man to plant fruit trees in the region. There is a restoration of three original mission buildings and three log structures have been moved here.

❧

LILLOOET: **Langford House** was built in 1878 by the town's storekeeper. The oldest residence in the B.C. interior, the wood frame structure has a mansard roof and gambrel windows. Mile 0, a cairn, marks the spot where, in 1859, construction began on the Old Cariboo Trail to the more northerly gold fields. In 1861-63 a road from Yale was built, bypassing Lillooet.

NELSON AREA

Sandon Ghost Town was founded in 1892 by Johnnie Harris. It turned into a boomtown when an acrobat, Eli Carpenter, who was climbing Mount Payne to look for a route for his circus to cross, discovered silver. Originally there were 24 hotels and saloons, gambling houses, an opera house, churches and a city hall. Today 18 are being restored, the others are left derelict.

❧

A street in Victoria

S.S. Moyie, Kaslo, Nelson area, the last of the Kootenay paddlewheelers, was built in Toronto in 1896 and shipped west in sections. Kaslo, where it is now located, was a supply centre in the 1890s for the silver boomtowns. The museum here contains the three-storey Langham Hotel, St. Andrew's Church, 1893, and a well-preserved city hall from 1898.

VANCOUVER & AREA

VANCOUVER has been described as having the most perfect location of any city in the world outside Rio de Janiero — the ocean, rivers and mountains create an idyllic setting. Its history is recent — the first white settlers didn't arrive until 1862.

Engine 374 was the first steam locomotive to pull a passenger train from Montreal to Vancouver. It arrived on May 23, 1887, and remained in service for over 55 years.

Old Hastings Mill Store is Vancouver's oldest building. The white clapboard building dates back to 1865 and is now a museum.

St. Roche National Historic Site is the home of the ship, built in 1928, that was the first to sail the Northwest Passage in both directions.

❧

Fort Langley National Historic Park was established in 1827 as a Hudson's Bay Company fort farther down river, but was moved to its present location in 1839; it burned and was rebuilt within a year. When James Douglas, an HBC officer, became the first governor of British Columbia he declared Fort Langley the colony's first capital. The fort has been partially restored to the 1850s period.

❧

HANEY: **St. John the Divine** is the oldest church in British Columbia. The Anglican church was built in 1858 at Derby and was moved here in 1882.

❧

Previous Pages
S.S. Moyie, Kaslo

Yale, The Fraser River

NEW WESTMINSTER: **Irving House** was built in 1862 by Captain William Irving. The 14-room, two-storey house has seven fireplaces, the original European wallpaper and 1860s Wilton carpets.

OTHER HISTORIC SITES

Anthony Island, Queen Charlotte Islands, holds an important collection of totem and mortuary poles of the Haida Indians. The village of Ninstints was occupied for about 2,000 years until abandoned in 1862, after a massacre of natives and a smallpox epidemic. Today 32 poles and the structural remains of 10 longhouses still exist here. This site is a unique example of the exuberance of coastal Indian culture.

❧

BARKERVILLE was the gold rush capital of the Cariboo. Gold was discovered on Williams Creek in 1862 and the town erupted almost overnight. It was destroyed by fire in 1868 and rebuilt. It has been restored as a living museum and includes a hotel and St. Saviour's Anglican Church.

❧

Cottonwood House, Barkerville area, is the only completely preserved roadhouse between Yale and Barkerville on the Cariboo Trail. It was built in 1864. The complex consists of an inn, stables and general store.

❧

BELLA COOLA: **Alexander Mackenzie Marker** is a rock in Dean Channel painted with the inscription "Alexander Mackenzie from Canada by land 22d July 1793." It commemorates the first crossing of North America north of Mexico.

❧

CROWSNEST PASS: **St. Joseph's Creek** was founded in 1874 by Oblate fathers. The residential school built in 1890, a 40-bed hospital (used during the typhoid epidemic that broke out during construction of the CPR's Crowsnest branch line) and church are still here. The church, built in 1893, a fine example of western Gothic architecture, has an ornate steeple.

❧

Fort St. James, Prince George area, was established in 1806 by Simon Fraser and John Stuart, explorers for the North West Company. In 1821, after

❧

Fort Yale

Main Street, Alert Bay

Inside of a house, Nootka Sound

Previous Pages
Old water wheel, originally used for gold mining, Fort Steele, near Kimberley

The Cameron Claim, Williams Creek, Cariboo

the North West Company merged with the Hudson's Bay Company, Fort St. James was the chief post in the area then known as New Caledonia. Five buildings from 1884 to 1889 are still standing, all fine examples of Red River and dovetailed log construction.

HAZELTON, Prince Rupert area, at the junction of the Skeena and Bulkley rivers, was an Indian village of great complexity when white men first arrived here in 1872. 'Ksan, a reproduction of that early Gitksan village, is a showplace of Indian culture from the region. It includes six cedar longhouses, plus totem poles, smokehouses and canoes.

KIMBERLEY AREA: **Fort Steele Historic Park** has restored buildings of the mid-1860s and reconstructions from the turn of the century. There are North West Mounted Police buildings, three churches, a vicarage, schoolhouse and the ferry office. The town originated as a ferry site during the 1885 gold rush that followed a strike at Wild Horse Creek.

KITWANGA, KITWANCOOL, KISPIOX, Prince Rupert area, are all within 64 km of Hazelton. They have the highest concentration of standing totem poles in the province. Kitwanga, a national historic site, contains archeological remains.

Overleaf
Church, Kitwanga Reserve, Hazelton
Trade Store, Fort Langley
'Ksan Indian Village, Hazelton